An Anthology of Essays on Cutting Edge Leadership

Dr. Joseph Mattera

Published by the independent self-publishing
platform CreateSpace.
www.createspace.com

ISBN 10: 1517499178
ISBN 13: 9781517499174

TABLE OF CONTENTS

PREFACE

This book arises out of almost four decades of my experiences in leadership roles in a local church and a nonprofit organization, regional and global networking, political and social engagement, and a regional and national network.

Since this is an anthology, some of the essays may allude to events that happened in the past or may give timelines of my leadership experience written over the last ten years.

The Essays

CHAPTER 1

Twelve Keys to Streamlining Your Focus

One of the biggest challenges for contemporary leaders arises from the large amount of available information. We not only have the challenge of information overload, but we also must sort through too many options and opportunities to make our organizations, ministries, and lives more effective. Leaders must learn to streamline their focus in order to maximize their potential.

Following are twelve principles regarding streamlining focus:

1. Tackle only one or two (at most) major areas in your life or organization at a time.

Depending on the season they are in, most human beings are capable of focusing on only one or two major things at once.

2. Understand the calling and mission of your organization.

Only invest your time with people, conferences, and resources that aid you in your distinct mission.

3. Understand your time limitations.

You may have a great real estate opportunity to increase your assets, but first you must determine whether you are called to manage more than you presently have on your plate.

4. Understand your gift limitations.

God calls us to do specific things based on our abilities. That is to say, we are not called to be involved in every opportunity that comes our way. Part of understanding our assignment comes from understanding our specific gift mix and staying within that framework of activity.

5. Know the geographic area of your influence.

God has called us to be married to the land. We have to determine what geographic area we are to focus on. For example, for a long time the apostle Peter stayed in Jerusalem because he was called to minister to Jewish people. The apostle Paul went to many nations because his call to the Gentiles was broader.

6. Know the demographic area you are called to.

Some are called to focus on children, some teens, some married couples, some seniors, etc. The sooner you understand your demographic call, the easier it will be to prioritize opportunities and open doors.

7. Listen for the voice of God in your soul when you are unsure what to work on first.

The Spirit bears witness in our spirit and leads us (Rom. 8:14–16).

8. Always prioritize getting the foundational things in order regarding leadership and legal issues.

We can only build a building as high as the foundation will allow it. The breadth of our reach will be determined by the depth of our base. If we want our influence to go beyond our present state, then we need to lay the right foundation.

9. Look for what is best, not merely for what is good for the leader or organization.

10. Receive counsel from key leadership and staff before making major alterations to your focus.

Proverbs teaches us to get much counsel before we go to war (Prov. 24:6, 15:22).

11. Remember that "a sale is not a sale" if you do not need the product.

Only invest your time and money in conferences, people, or information resources that you either need immediately or that will get you to the next level of your assignment.

12. Invest the bulk of your time only with those you are assigned to build the kingdom with.

Many people diffuse their focus because they waste much of their time hanging out with friends for momentary pleasure and neglect their long-term purposes.

CHAPTER 2

Why All Leaders Need to Be Followers

We have an unhealthy church culture in which people in ministry and leadership often believe they are above what they sing and preach. For example, many worship-team members and leaders habitually go hang out somewhere in the church building after they "perform" and do not sit under the word. Also, many elders and leaders in the typical local church lead small groups, preach, or do both, but do not have a place in the church for personal ministry and accountability. Also, lead pastors often preach accountability and submission to authority but have no one outside their local church that speaks into their lives.

Following are five dangerous attitudes that lead to rebellion (Isa. 14:12–15):
Rebellion is the "sin principle" in which all other sins, including pride, are manifest.

1. Isolation

Isolation is, in this context, cutting yourself off in your heart and mind from allowing other people to speak into your life. For example, you can be physically present in a meeting but emotionally disconnected from the voices of those around you. Just because you attend church and leadership meetings does not mean you are not isolating yourself. The fact is when you shut yourself down emotionally from others and refuse to walk in honesty and transparency, you are isolating yourself. Extreme cases of isolation manifest in a person cutting him- or herself off from a local church, but the former (more subtle) form of isolation is where it begins.

Isaiah 14:12–15 shows how Lucifer kept on saying "I" before he led the rebellion against God. Whenever you think of "I" and not "we" and "us," you are beginning to get into dangerous territory.

2. Autonomy

Autonomy is, in this context, when your isolation leads you to reject all authority over your life. Whenever people shut themselves down emotionally from their overseer, they are beginning the process of rejecting their authority, thus setting themselves up as the lone authority. Isaiah 14:14 shows that Lucifer's isolation eventually led to him making himself equal with the most high God in his heart.

3. Division

Whenever a person, especially a secondary leader in a local church, makes him- or herself equal in authority to the lead pastor, division is not far behind. Lucifer went from being one of God's most trusted archangels to leading a rebellion against God. Isaiah 14:14 shows that he tried to make himself equal with God, and Revelation 12:4, 7–9 shows how that led to rebellion against the authority of God.

If Satan was audacious enough to attempt to bring rebellion against God, how much more will he try to bring rebellion and insurrection against a local church? There is only one vision in every church. Any secondary leaders who have their own visions that do not point to the visions of their churches are drawing disciples away unto themselves (Acts 20:30), and they are already causing division, which means two visions (even if there is not yet slander or gossip).

4. Uncovering the Leader (Gen. 9:20–27)

All leaders are fallen sinners. Nobody is perfect. When you see a fault in a leader, it is an opportunity to pray for him or her and walk in Matthew 18:15–17. If it is a serious sin like heretical teaching, fraud, adultery, or abuse, then you should tell one of the elders and ask for a hearing to confront the pastor or bishop. If none of the leaders agrees with you, and you are convinced there is serious error, then leave the church as quietly as possible. Leave it to God to judge.

When all is said and done, we need to deal with the weaknesses and sins of our leaders with an attitude of covering their sins instead of humiliating and uncovering them. The son of Noah who uncovered him (Ham) was cursed for generations. The other two sons, who walked backward and covered their father's nakedness, were blessed for generations. In the same way, David never killed King Saul when he had the chance, because he did not want to touch God's anointed. He said, let God judge him. In our context, uncovering can be slandering, gossiping, backbiting, complaining, and using body language—anything meant to undermine and belittle the authority of the leader over your life.

5. Rebellion

Rebellion is when we outright reject any spiritual authority over our lives. This can come as a result of arrogance (thinking we know more than our leaders), unforgiveness, bitterness, or a hurt inflicted in your mind by the leader. Rebellion against God-given leadership is really rebellion against God (Matt. 10:40) and will lead to a severe divine correction.

Setting up leadership the way God instructed us

In Numbers 11:11–17 we find that God told Moses to choose the seventy elders who would lead the congregation of Israel. God then took of the spirit that was on Moses and put it upon those elders. This is profound because if God was the one who chose the elders, then the elders could bypass Moses and go directly to God, thus undermining Moses's authority.

Also, God did not just put His Spirit on the elders; he took of Moses's spirit—which was a combination of Moses's life experience, character, vision, anointing, and spiritual DNA—with the Holy Spirit and put it upon those elders, so the vision and calling of the nation would continue. Hence, all leaders should carry the same corporate anointing God put upon their visionary leader in order to see the purpose of the congregation come to pass.

Furthermore, in Numbers 27:20 Moses had to lay hands upon Joshua and impart his authority to him in order for the congregation to obey him.

In the New Testament, Ephesians 4:7–12 teaches us that grace to be empowered for service doesn't come directly from heaven, but through the grace already given to the fivefold minister you are sitting under. Thus, grace for salvation comes directly from heaven, but grace for ministry comes from God through the ministry's gifts to the church.

Finally, Ephesians 4:15–16 shows that every member in the body of Christ should be in a place to receive ministry, including the lead pastor, bishop, or apostle. The lead pastor should be able to have regular leadership meetings for mutual edification in his or her local church. He or she should also have an overseer outside the local church who speaks into his or her life, holds him or her accountable, and can be called upon by the church elders in case of an emergency or when serious charges are brought against him or her.

May God give us a healthy church culture in which all leaders become followers of other leaders, who also have leaders speaking into their lives.

CHAPTER 3

Why Great Leaders Must Suffer More Than Others

One day I was pondering why all the leaders I know with much influence seem to have one thing in common: they have all suffered much in their lives. In fact, every one of them has a particular cross to bear, or they have gone through horrendous seasons of pain and suffering that were part of a divine process that made them and continues to mold them into the highly effective leaders they are today. (These challenges can be relational issues with their spouses, children, other leaders, etc., or they can be personal issues related to their spiritual, emotional, or physical well-being.)

We see this illustrated in Acts 9 when God tells Ananias that Paul would have to suffer much for the name of Jesus (Acts 9:16). We can read Paul's own testimony about himself regarding the reason for his suffering in 2 Corinthians 12:1–10:

> I must go on boasting. Though there is nothing to be gained by it, I will go on to visions and revelations of the Lord. I know a man in Christ who fourteen years ago was caught up to the third heaven—whether in the body or out of the body I do not know, God knows. And I know that this man was caught up into paradise—whether in the body or out of the body I do not know, God knows—and he heard things that cannot be told, which man may not utter. On behalf of this man I will boast, but on my own behalf I will not boast, except of my weaknesses—though if I should wish to boast, I would not be a fool, for I would be speaking the truth; but I refrain from it, so that no one may think more of me than he sees in me or hears from me. So to keep me from becoming conceited because of the surpassing greatness of

the revelations, a thorn was given me in the flesh, a messenger of Satan to harass me, to keep me from becoming conceited. Three times I pleaded with the Lord about this, that it should leave me. But he said to me, "My grace is sufficient for you, for my power is made perfect in weakness." Therefore I will boast all the more gladly of my weaknesses, so that the power of Christ may rest upon me. For the sake of Christ, then, I am content with weaknesses, insults, hardships, persecutions, and calamities. For when I am weak, then I am strong.

According to this passage, Paul's suffering was connected to his leadership ability and great calling, which had to be tempered through his suffering because our human sin nature has a propensity to boast about our own accomplishments. God has to allow pain in our lives to keep us dependent upon Him because all of us are born in sin with the fleshly tendencies to brag about our own accomplishments and trust in our own gifts, abilities, and flesh instead of in His grace.

As I view my own life and the lives of others I know personally, I can see how the very things that make us successful are also connected to our sin nature, which has been the root of much sin in our lives. For example, in my own life, the stubbornness, perseverance, and tendency to move forward for the sake of Christ in spite of all obstacles is connected to how I coped with rejection, isolation, and pain in childhood. Namely, I made a name for myself by excelling in street fighting, sports, music, and in other areas of life—all to carve out a name and identity for myself so I would be praised, respected, and celebrated by my peers. Although this developed in me qualities of perseverance in the midst of pain and suffering, it was for my glory and not for God's glory!

Thus, the development of qualities I use to this day as part of my leadership portfolio, my gifts and abilities, are directly connected to the habits or patterns I developed out of my sin nature and my desire to carve out a name for myself for the sake of self-worth and self-esteem. This shows me that God even used my sins for His glory!

In summary, the gifts and abilities I use today as a leader in the body of Christ were originally inspired, molded, and developed in the fiery furnace of self-survival in my childhood, and they all emanated out of a desire to make a name for myself and not for the Lord Jesus Christ! So my gifts and calling are inextricably connected to the very sin nature Jesus had to die for! This is why God has to continually allow great challenges, pain, and suffering in my life as a way of tempering my tendency to depend upon myself, honor myself, and trust in myself for results!

The greater the leader, the more stubborn he or she has to be to resist temptation, to stay focused, and to be successful, even though this same stubbornness may have originally developed and emanated out of his or her personal rebellion against God before he or she was saved! Thus, there is always a fine line between our great leadership qualities and our sinful tendencies to rebel against God and build our own kingdoms! (This also explains why great leaders often fall into scandal, especially if they allow their hectic schedules to crowd out their continual need for spiritual formation in God's presence.)

Going back to the apostle Paul: as he matured, he actually bragged more about his weaknesses than his accomplishments so the power of Christ could rest on him! What a far cry from some of today's preachers who are constantly bragging about how much victory, power, and accomplishments they have in their ministries! In reality, the more spiritually immature leaders are, the more they will brag about accomplishments; the more mature they are, the more they will brag about their weaknesses and glorify Christ's grace that empowers them!

Finally, understanding these concepts should help us in two areas. First, instead of discouraging leaders, this should be a great source of encouragement, since many leaders suffer silently because they are embarrassed and think they are the only leaders continually dealing with painful issues—something Satan can use to cause a leader to quit out of sheer discouragement and a sense of failure. Leaders should take heart and know that they are not alone in their pain. To the extent a leader has influence, he or she will have to endure the process of pain so his or her gifts and abilities can be continually redeemed for the glory and honor of God.

Second, the key to discovering and dealing with the dominant sin issues in our lives is to honestly reflect on our talents, gifts, and abilities and on how we have trusted in them to manipulate others, control our environments for self-autonomy, and carve out names for ourselves. This is similar to how Lucifer attempted to do the same when his pride motivated him to try to exalt himself above the throne of God for self-autonomy and self-glorification (Isa. 14:12–14).

Understanding this enables us to have a greater understanding and appreciation for the depths and riches of the love and grace of God, who loves us and even uses the very abilities that have been connected to our self-glorification, fleshly preservation, and desires to carve out names for ourselves. This tendency must constantly be checked with challenges, obstacles, and the issues of life. God surrounds power with problems so that, by the time we have power and influence, we have become so broken, humble, and dependent upon God that we would not be so quick to share the glory with God for the great accomplishments that arise out of our feeble efforts!

CHAPTER 4

Ten Significant Power Principles for Effective, Sustainable Leadership

If you want to grow a church or organization, grow the leader! The following power principles maximize effectiveness, as I've learned during my more than three decades of church and marketplace ministry.

1. Focus

By far, one of the greatest death knells to gifted leaders is their lack of focus! I have found that the more gifted a person is, the more he or she is tempted to accomplish more things than he or she has the capacity to properly manage. Most of the time, less is more! Most people are only going to excel at a very few things. To be effective, focus on your strengths, delegate the rest, and remember to always "keep the main thing the main thing"!

2. Develop a Brand

Branding is almost as important as content and quality! You are no good to the world if no one knows why you exist!

For example, it is important that all itinerant speakers be known for specific areas of teaching based on their expertise, even if they can speak well on other topics. All marketing strategies should employ strategies to connect your name to your primary calling and assignment. For example, years ago, if I thought of a faith teacher, the name Kenneth Hagin would immediately come to mind; if I thought of cell groups, it would trigger the name David Yonggi Cho; presently, John Maxwell comes to mind when I think of leadership. In my circles, regarding strategy, John Kelly comes to mind.

As a local church pastor, I have had to teach on many different things, but as an itinerant minister, I will only travel out of town to minister if I can teach either on the Kingdom of God or on leadership development. Consequently, I have now been branded with my life message (the lordship of Christ over all spheres of life) because of my articles and because the first four books I have written are on the Kingdom of God (which was my intention). I can teach on numerous subjects from scripture, but I would usually not fly halfway around the world to teach if I could not teach topics based upon my primary assignment in life.

3. Incorporate a Think Tank

The more responsibility and opportunity he or she has, the more an effective leader will have to incorporate either an informal or formal think tank in regards to future decisions and opportunities. The book of Proverbs teaches us that in the abundance of counselors we make war! King Rehoboam failed because he did not have a seasoned and wise think tank around him (1 Kings 11)!

I have found that the more opportunities that arise, the more efficient my capacity must be to match those opportunities, or I will eventually become the bottleneck of my own assignment! The best way to streamline future decision-making processes is to have in place various committees or circles of advisors that can help you discern whether an opportunity is wheat or chaff.

4. Belong to a "Power Community"

Every leader needs to be continually inspired, encouraged, and even challenged by others. One of the best ways is to find a small community of like-minded leaders (friends) with a similar trajectory who are called to partner or collaborate with you. The importance of this "power community" cannot be overstated for long-term success. Lonely and isolated leaders usually lack

the long-term passion and knowledge needed to fulfill
their purposes.

5. Recruit a Benefactor Team

If a leader does not have money, his or her vision is
nothing more than an unfulfilled dream! As we read the
book of Acts, we see that many of the people who
traveled with the apostle Paul supported him financially.
In Luke 8 we find that a group of wealthy women
followed Jesus and supported His itinerant ministry.
Every leader has to recruit a benefactor team made up of
people gifted with wealth creation and business acumen
so that the leader can focus fully on the implementation
of his or her vision instead of wasting emotional energy
worrying about having sufficient funds.

6. Sharpen the Axe

If an axe is dull, the person wielding it will work very
hard with few results! In the same way, an effective
leader needs to take time out for spiritual, emotional, and
physical renewal. We need to keep our core values of
faith and family at the center of our lives and never
neglect them for our work. We also need to have a
healthy balance of work and play so we do not
experience emotional burnout and work-related fatigue.
It is good to be "weary in the work," but it is never good
to be "weary of the work"! Many leaders are so busy
their bodies are continually trying to catch up to their
souls while they are running on emotional fumes!
Leaders like this usually start off great but have a
difficult time finishing the race!

7. Prioritize Integrity

Leaders are called to build their lives upon character
and integrity and never merely upon their gifts and
abilities! The more trustworthy a leader is, the more

other people will trust him or her, which will increase his or her overall influence and impact! It is vital in this day of scandal and hypocrisy that leaders integrate their private faith with their public persona and service. When leaders speak one way and live another way, their dualism will eventually damage their work and families! Only transformed leaders can truly transform their surroundings!

8. Strive for Humility

In this context, *humility* means to think of your gifts, abilities, and calling in a realistic way. Humility is not putting yourself down or thinking of yourself higher than you ought to think but being honest with yourself. Hence, the more humble a person is, the more self-aware he or she becomes. Only self-aware people can truly focus properly since they do not suffer grandeurs of delusion and are not legends in their own minds; they are able to spend time effectively and selectively in the areas of their calling.

Conversely, proud and presumptuous people are constantly running around trying to please and impress every person who "blows in their ear"!

9. Value Justice

Effective leaders are going to live their lives based on living a just life. This means, they will be fair to everyone under their influence or in their organizations. They do not allow ungodly prejudice and bias to sway their emotions and distort their treatment of others.

By *justice*, I do not mean egalitarianism or forced equality and entitlements because, when we give people something they don't deserve, they don't appreciate it and trample it under their feet!

10. Embody Love in Everything You Do

The Bible teaches us in 1 Corinthians 13 that the greatest of all the attributes is love! Love is patient and kind, is not boastful or arrogant, is not self-seeking; without love we are nothing and have nothing, no matter how successful we are in the eyes of the world. Therefore, the greatest power principle of all in regards to leadership is love. Hence, it behooves us as leaders to continually integrate the love of God and neighbor into our every word, deed, action, and goals so that, at the end of the day, we will hear the voice of the master say to us, "Well done, my faithful servant"!

CHAPTER 5

Understanding the Differences between Protégés, Partners, and Parasites

Having been involved with pastoral and apostolic-type ministry for more than three decades, I have attempted to prioritize building relationally through covenant and through mentoring. This experience has shown me that, in order to be successful, I must distinguish among three types of people: protégés, partners, and parasites.

The following are my observations regarding these three kinds of people:

Protégés:

By *protégé* I mean someone I am mentoring who is open to growing with a heart to serve together with me for the kingdom. Usually it is a younger emerging leader in whom I see leadership potential, which motivates me to invest my time into him or her.

The greatest call upon my life is to mentor and nurture the next generation of leaders so that the influence of God's kingdom can penetrate every facet of society. In order for me to accomplish this, there has to be a generational impact in which the next generation of leaders is equipped to stand upon the shoulders of those leaders who preceded them.

A protégé would develop a deep relationship of trust with me, have access to me, and allow me to speak into his or her life. In many cases, we have to choose our successors in every aspect of our life's work; our successors will most likely arise out of the pool of protégés we are mentoring. That being said, I am constantly looking for potential protégés to pour into; some will be short term for a season, and some will have a lifetime relationship with me. Discovering a divine connection with a new protégé is one of the great joys of my life!

Partners:

In order to establish kingdom influence in a community, city, or nation, we have to establish many partnerships. No leader, organization, or church will be able to bring societal transformation by him- or herself!

Another great joy in my life is when God connects me in peer relationships with other like-minded leaders who have high levels of influence in their particular spheres.

For example, in the word of God, we find that in order to rebuild Jerusalem during the postexilic era, God partnered together two men: Nehemiah, a politician who received a government grant and safe passage from the Persian king for his assignment to rebuild the walls of Jerusalem, and Ezra, a religious leader who taught the word of God to those repatriating back into Jerusalem from exile. In my more than three decades of ministry, I would not have been able to accomplish much in the way of church and marketplace ministry if I had not collaborated with key leaders in both spheres.

Partners must have a certain amount of influence depending upon the task at hand. They must have willing hearts to serve, be trustworthy, have no hidden agendas, and be willing to do what it takes to get the job done. If they are all talk and no action, I cannot count upon them to be partners.

Parasites:

Last, but not least, there will always be parasites who want to use your name, influence, authority, and gifting to benefit themselves while not having a mutual motivation to benefit you. The scientific definition of *parasite* can come in handy here: a parasite is "an organism that grows, feeds, and is sheltered on or in a different organism while contributing nothing to the survival of its host." Thus, in this context, a parasite is someone who feeds off of other people to sustain him- or herself, while not reciprocating a mutual benefit.

Of course, some are not in a position to have a mutually beneficial relationship with anyone, such as young natural children and newly born spiritual children, as well as some people in trauma. But, in the context of this essay, I am using *parasite* to refer to a person who should be in a position to have mutually beneficial relationships, but, because he or she is self-focused, only relates to those he or she can take advantage of, since the person's only agenda is self-preservation, self-aggrandizement, or both! Parasites have no motivation to give blessings back, even though they may talk a good talk.

These are the people who drop names to get ahead, who use your influence to get what they want, and who will feign friendship with you as long as you are doing something for them!

Consequently, if at all possible, avoid these kinds of people, and do not waste your time investing into them (except to win them to Christ) because, unless they change, they will go from one relationship to another and never bear long-lasting fruit for the kingdom! Their very nature, motivation, and behavior totally repel the attitude of the Lord Jesus who came not to serve but to serve and give His life as a ransom for many (Matt. 20:28)!

In closing, not every person in the body of Christ has the same motivations, maturity levels, goals, and emotional health levels. This is why we need to properly discern between the above three kinds of people. If we do not, we will try to make a parasite a protégé or make a protégé a partner prematurely, and we will experience much failure and frustration in our lives!

CHAPTER 6

Reasons for the Rise and Fall of Leaders

Scripture is replete with examples of how leaders rise and fall. One of the reasons I believe the Bible is the inspired word of God is because it so honestly and accurately portrays the plight of human beings regarding their reasons for success and failures. It adequately portrays the dark side of the saints of old and is not like the common biographies of great people in history that are more hagiographic in nature than historic (that is, they don't reveal the failures of the person).

From what I have observed, many, if not most, leaders do not end well. The following reasons have to do with long-lasting success or failure. Some leaders may experience both for a short period but not end up that way in the long term.

Reasons for the Rise of Leaders:

The following are eleven reasons why leaders are promoted by God for lifelong effectiveness:

1. They are promoted by God to be used by God to complete a particular assignment.

God promotes whom He chooses (Ps. 75:6–7). There is no other explanation. We know some folks who are very effective and very godly leaders who are not very well known. Then, there are well-known leaders who are not very effective or godly. It is a divine mystery as to why God gives some people more of a public platform than others. As Paul said, no person should boast or brag as if he or she has elevated him- or herself; everything we have received has come from God. Thus, we should not be jealous of others or become worried about the amount of influence we have (Prov. 3:5–7; 1 Cor. 4:7; 2 Cor. 10:12–18).

2. They have learned to live lives of brokenness and dependence on God instead of living lives based on their own strengths and giftedness.

I have been in full-time ministry for almost thirty years, and I have found that the true people of God who have a track record of long-time success all have one thing in common: they have allowed the Lord to break their strong wills and soften their stubborn hearts. Like Jacob of old, they walk with a limp (Gen. 32:24–31). Anyone who has allowed God to deal with him or her will walk with a limp. I don't trust any leader who doesn't walk with a limp!

3. They have learned from the lessons of the past.

All of us will go through great challenges in our lives. The book of Proverbs tells us that a person who accepts correction is wise (10:8), but a fool refuses correction (15:5). In the arena of life, not only will wise people like our parents or pastors attempt to correct us, but the situations of life will also be orchestrated by God so that we are conformed to His image (Rom. 8:28–30). The wise person learns from both people and life experience and doesn't repeat serious mistakes.

4. They have learned from the lessons of what others have experienced.

Effective leaders do a lot of reading of other successful leaders and do a lot of listening when in the company of wise, great leaders. We have to do more listening than speaking and make time to fellowship with great minds by reading the books of those we want to emulate.

5. They get adequate counsel.

Proverbs teaches us that before we go to war, we need an abundance of counsel. To be effective you must learn to hire staff based on your weaknesses, while concentrating on your areas of expertise and strength. The smartest people in the world are those who know and have access to the smartest people they can possibly surround themselves with.

6. They have adequate coaching and mentoring in specific areas of need.

I have an inner circle of people and receive coaching in numerous areas of my life. I don't have the time to read every available book or get every available degree, so I constantly receive coaching and mentoring from others with more expertise than I have in areas like administration, finances, law, nutrition, health, emotional well-being, marriage and relationships, etc. If I didn't have people who constantly coached me, then I would be a disaster and would greatly limit my leadership ceiling!

7. They are accountable to others.

If you desire long-lasting success, then you must have accountability regarding your finances, marriage, personal relationships, how you do ministry, strategic planning, and the like. Because all of us have a dark side, we need to have open relationships with people God has assigned to us and give permission to speak correction into our lives.

8. They live a balanced life that includes emotional and physical health.

Jesus was both human and divine. Many of us forget that we must take care of our emotional and physical health, not just run on spiritual fumes and anointing! We are called to love our neighbor even as we love ourselves. If we do not care for ourselves, we will burn out and not be able to be a blessing to others! We need to set physical and emotional boundaries that limit our activities and what we say yes to, so that we will remain a blessing to our families and have time to minister to the Lord for self-renewal.

9. They know how to read, interpret, and discern the hearts of other key people around them.

This is not something that can be taught. Great leaders have an intangible, intuitive ability to read other people accurately. They usually know whom to trust and whom to partner with. Often, they can tell when God is connecting them to someone instantly, even without meeting that person before!

10. They have a heart after God more than a desire for promotion and ministry.

For long-lasting success we need to come to a place where we truly desire to seek God and know God more than making Him known! Only then can God trust us.

11. They have prudence in the governance of their ministry.

A person once told me that he heard that Billy Graham had met with his team members many years ago and decided on certain core principles they would always follow for the success of their ministry:
  a. Pursue excellence in administration (vision without administration is only a pipe dream!).
  b. Never be alone with a woman you are not married to.
  c. Never exaggerate. (They vowed to call their ministry what it really was. If there were 50 people in a meeting, then they would say publicly that there were 50 people at the meeting; they wouldn't say there were 150 people.)

d. Have financial scrutiny and integrity. Hiring outside independent auditors as if they were IRS agents checking the ministry's books is something all leaders should do on an annual basis.

Reasons for the Fall of Leaders:

1. They live out of their natural giftedness and spiritual anointing but do not build on character and integrity.

First Corinthians teaches that the Corinthian church lacked no gift (1:7), yet its members were also carnal, acting like mere babes in Christ (3:1–4). It is no accident that, after the great chapter describing the manifestations of the Spirit (12), the next chapter is fully devoted to love (13). Paul says that if we have faith that can move mountains but have not love, we are nothing! Matthew 7:21–23 tells us that we can do miracles and still miss the kingdom of heaven! We need to focus on living a life in which the love of God is fully integrated into our character and habit patterns. This is the only way we can build a long-lasting foundation.

2. They have not learned how to process pain.

Because leaders are targets and often experience betrayal, they need to learn to give adequate time to process the pain they feel when someone leaves their church or organization. If we do not fully process and face our pain, then these unresolved issues will spill over and cause anger, resentment, sarcasm, and bitterness that seep into our lives, cause great dysfunction, and cut off the ability for ministry longevity. We have to learn to grieve, mourn, and process pain until we fully face it and fully forgive before we move on to the next phase of our lives and relationships.

3. They are emotionally immature in certain areas of their lives.

Any area of our lives in which we were traumatized will cause us to stop growing emotionally until we actually face the trauma and allow the Lord to release us from it and heal our hearts. Often this means we also have to forgive folks, whether they are still alive or dead. Any age of our life in which we have not adequately dealt with and resolved trauma will hinder us from progressing emotionally. This is why a person can be forty years old and have the emotional maturity of a five-year-old in a particular area of his or her life.

4. They are quick to form an opinion and judge others.

5. They are not aware of their dark side and so live in self-deception.

We purposely allow areas of discomfort to be rationalized away or pushed aside so we can paint our own picture of ourselves, our worth, and our ministries. Often, the reality of who we think we are does not line up with who God made us to be. Exhibition A is watching the tryouts for *American Idol*. Some people have no skill in singing, and yet they are convinced, based on years of dreaming certain things, that they will one day become a superstar. Simon Cowell of *American Idol* may have been rude and blunt, but at least he gave people a dose of reality!

6. They live for the future and are never living in the present.

Many leaders live miserable lives because they are always yearning for something more. Unfortunately, they are never really living in the present but only in past regrets and the future. Thus, they never stop to enjoy and appreciate the people around them.

Instead, they often attempt to leverage people so they can reach their illustrious "future." I am sick and tired of some of the prophecies that come forth about some glorious future that may or may not come to pass in our lifetime. I think we also need prophecies that get us to appreciate what God has already done and who God has put in our lives today so we can begin to maximize our gifts and release our great potential. If we don't appreciate what God is doing in the present, He can't trust us with a more glorious future (1 Thess. 5:16, 18)!

7. They use people instead of loving people.

Many are the leaders who view the people around them merely as objects to serve in the church—to tithe or to be some kind of blessing to bring them and their organization to the next level. God is looking for leaders who will celebrate and not exploit the people He has entrusted to them!

8. They have a heart for ministry more than a heart for God.

Those who only seek God or study the Bible to preach a message are truly missing it. I have found that when I seek God just to delight in Him, He pours amazing messages into me for the church and gives me all the strategy I need to go to the next level. God chose King David because he was a man after God's heart!

9. They do not receive correction or coaching from others.

I have been with leaders who did not want to hear any negative things about their lives or ministries. Hence, they never grew and often failed and left their positions in Christ. We need each other not only for moral support, but also so we can effectively hear from God as a hermeneutical community. Those who can learn from the community of people God has surrounded them with will grow the fastest. This is one of the things I admire so much about Bill Hybels. He radically changed the way he did church based on an honest church survey that he calls "REVEAL." If he wasn't open to hearing from God from his community, then he would still be attempting to employ unsuccessful strategies to make disciples in his local church today.

10. They seek and need the approval of men more than the approval of God.

Many who are involved in ministry have never dealt with the need for approval from a father who abandoned them. Thus, they are ministering more out of a need for respect and affirmation than to please God. Consequently, they will live without personal boundaries and say yes to numerous ministry endeavors that God didn't command them to do. They will also push their churches to fund projects more because they desire a monument that points to the success in their lives than because they are motivated to expand the Kingdom of God. These leaders often burn out and have terrible family relationships because, ultimately, they are "driven" and are not being "led" by the spirit of Christ.

CHAPTER 7

Thirty Years, Thirty Leadership Lessons

Thirty years ago this week, my wife, Joyce, and I traveled to the Soviet Union for six weeks on a three-city missionary tour. This began a process culminating in our official launch into full-time church ministry in November 1980.

During our thirty years of ministry, we held numerous evangelistic events that saw thousands give their lives to Christ; we founded a growing and very influential local church; we participated in the founding of a children's charity that serves thousands of at-risk children; we started a coalition for apostolic leaders and pastors; we started a large network of pastors overseas; and we spoke at hundreds of leadership conferences in many different nations. After looking back and reflecting upon those years, I wrote down the the top thirty lessons I have learned so I can pass them on to other leaders. As a bonus, I included six other important pieces of advice that all church leaders would be wise to heed.

1. Spend time with God before meeting man (Acts 6:1–4 Exod. 18:19–23).

Some pastors become hyphenated pastor-deacons because they spend more time in administration than in the word and prayer.

Up until thirty years ago, most pastors worked out of a study because they spent much of their time reading and praying. Now pastors (including me) work out of our offices because our primary work is administration and strategy. A lot of this cannot be helped in smaller churches and because the world we live in today is very complicated. But we still need to strike a balance and at least spend our mornings studying and seeking God before we go to our offices.

The early church and Moses of the first covenant were powerful because their first line of business was to be "Godward" so they could adequately enunciate God's word to their congregations.

2. Prioritize time with my wife and children before ministry opportunities.

I fill my calendar first with vacation time with my family before I plan anything else. This guarantees my time with them is protected.

Nothing stresses me out more than when my relationships with my wife and children are out of whack. Truly, Satan gets the biggest foothold into the lives of leaders by destroying their families. When we neglect our spouses because of overworking in the church, our ministry becomes our mistress! When we neglect our children for the work of the Lord, then our children become resentful toward God and church and fall away from their kingdom purpose!

3. Prioritize my time in the local church, nurturing those with leadership potential.

My ministry focus has always centered around 2 Timothy 2:2, in which Paul instructs Timothy to prioritize spending time pouring into those who would be able to teach others and are faithful.

This is more important than counseling, hospital visits, or running around putting out fires.

I find that I cannot pastor effectively unless I have leaders who will help bear the load.

4. Develop a strong administrative team.

Anointing to preach and lead inspires and gathers people, but only the creation of systems grows and stabilizes a church.

Many great leaders have small churches because they haven't created systems for shepherding church members, managing finances, meeting with small groups, and establishing discipleship programs.

5. Reach out and network with key pastors in your city.

There is only one church but many congregations in every city and community. Hence, it behooves us to get to know and partner with key pastors and churches in our communities. If we don't do this, we become islands and will not properly discern the body of Christ in our cities. (First Corinthians 11:27–30 shows that often there is a lack of apostolic power in our churches because of all the divisions in the church.)

6. Get involved in the civic leadership of your local community.

My influence for the Gospel greatly multiplied when I showed care for the practical needs of my community by joining the local community board, aiding the NYPD, and giving counsel to key political and community leaders.

Also, these leaders turned out to be incredible blessings to our church, helping us with zoning and other important issues related to the logistics of operating a large ministry in a complicated city like New York.

7. Obtain influence by serving others.

One of the most important lessons I have learned is that "he or she who serves leads." When we try to push our own agenda on people, they will back away and become suspicious of us. But when we are concerned with the agenda of others and are willing to serve them, we gain influence. Jesus said the greatest in the kingdom is the one who serves (Mark 10:43).

8. Have a holistic approach to ministry and enhance the quality of life in your community instead of offering mere words.

The church is called to glorify God the Father by our good works (Matthew 5:16).
When a church meets a felt material or social need in its community and contributes to enhancing the quality of life for the population, it gains great influence and respect. When most people in a community don't even know that a particular local church exists or don't think the church is relevant, then it has not been functioning as the salt of the earth and light of the world.

The main reason why community boards are now blocking churches from obtaining the best real estate and fighting their tax-exempt statuses is because the primary reason for tax exemption is that churches were deemed benefits to the quality of life for their communities. When churches only offer good preaching, they are not deemed relevant and are at risk in our post-Christian America of being stripped of their most favored tax status.

9. Develop a personal mission statement that will aid you in choosing which events to participate in.

I get so many offers to attend meetings and speak at conferences that I must have a strong base of core values and priorities based on my mission that serves as a grid that narrows the ministry opportunities I will take.

10. Develop close mentoring friendships with specific people representing church, business, law, health, and politics.

As a pastor I could have a narrow view of the world if all I did was socialize with other Christians and pastors. In order to be effective, I need to have a strong inner circle of people who are experts in various realms of life.

11. Engage in life-giving activities outside of ministry for mental and emotional renewal.

When you are involved with the same thing (even ministry) over and over again, it drains you emotionally and mentally. I have to renew myself with activities outside of church ministry by doing things I love, such as playing my guitar, exercising, and having fun with friends.

12. Prioritize eating a healthy diet and getting regular exercise.

Eating healthy and staying in top physical shape enables a leader to have great amounts of mental, spiritual, and physical energy to fulfill vision. Those who are continually getting sick and are run down and tired because of their diets and poor heath are poor stewards of the life God has given them.

13. Get enough sleep and take regular time off for prayer, study, and reflection

I have found that I can't think clearly unless I get away regularly for several days at a time to pray and hear God's voice for my life. When I don't do this, I easily get lost emotionally because I don't give my body enough time to process challenging events in my life. This results in me getting off-center.

14. Take your leadership and key people away on retreats on a regular basis to pour into them and develop community.

I have found that a one-day seminar involving fellowship and reflection does more to bring unity and vision than many meetings over the course of several months.

15. Develop leadership communities built around friendship, covenant, and kingdom purpose instead of only having meetings centered on teaching and agendas.

When we have meetings that minister to the personal needs of those who serve in leadership, we will actually get more work done than if we just meet to discuss problems and go over our ministry agendas. Eventually people get worn out attending meetings, but when they are renewed and refreshed in a meeting, they can't wait to come back for more!

16. Love and appreciate every person, whether or not he or she is serving and benefiting your local church or ministry.

17. Attempt to keep a good relationship with every person who leaves your local church or ministry.

Unfortunately, many pastors take it personally and even blackball those who have left their churches, possibly for fear they will influence others to leave. I have found the best thing to do in the sight of God is to continue to love and reach out to those who have left, even if they have no plans of ever coming back!

This keeps love flowing in the body of Christ, and it is Christ honoring when we put His kingdom first!

18. Have a top finance manager and CPA managing the tithes and offerings.

Since most pastors are not equipped to properly oversee the accounting of a church or organization, the highest priority should be given to hiring a competent CPA and then a skilled and trustworthy finance manager. When the finances are not managed well, it opens up a satanic door for scandals and can dry up the tithes and offerings faster than any other accusation!

19. To get more work done, make a distinction and have some elders who focus only on the spiritual aspects of the vision and other elders who focus only on the finances meeting regularly in separate committees.

20. Purchase your own church property as soon as possible.

Our local church didn't really have its greatest influence in our community until we were able to purchase our own property. Having our own property has enabled us to greatly establish and expand our ministry and has given our church a greater sense of stability and respect in our community. Renting limited our ministry capacity because we couldn't set our own hours and could only meet a few days per week.

21. Save at least 10 percent of all monies that are collected in case of financial emergencies.

For the longest time, our church donated 10 percent of the congregational tithes to other ministries and saved another 10 percent in a reserve account in case of emergencies. Functioning on 80 percent of our weekly offerings allows us to be wise in how we spend our money and has proved to be one of the smartest things we have ever done!

22. The senior pastor should start preparing the next generation of leaders and prepare their potential successors when they reach forty-five years of age.

Numbers 8:23–26 teaches that priests are to serve between the ages of twenty-five and fifty. Then, at age fifty, priests should retire and only assist (and mentor) the younger priests. This forces a continual flow of generational continuity and demands that young folks start getting trained to serve, probably in their early teenage years.

It is a shame and unbiblical when we see older pastors (sixty and over) serving with no plan for succession.

23. Have a strong presbytery of apostolic leaders you submit to for counsel and in case of an emergency.

I tell independent evangelical pastors they need to submit to an overseer and belong to an organization for mutual support, accountability, and input. This is something like fire insurance—in case a scandal breaks out and they need someone to come in and mediate between them and their congregations.

24. Plan seasonal campaigns to keep up the momentum in the ministry.

For starters, you can take advantage of the already established Christian calendar that has served the body of Christ well for over two thousand years (Christmas, Lent, Easter, Pentecost Sunday, etc.).
Often we will have a momentum-creating event (like Easter Sunday or an anniversary) but nothing to follow up the event, and we lose any momentum that was created. This is like a plane using half of its energy to gain altitude to thirty thousand feet and then running out of fuel and diving back to the ground!

25. Never make important decisions regarding a relationship or the ministry while you are angry, tired, depressed, or frustrated.

Many relationships have ended because of an e-mail sent out in haste or in anger.

26. Understand that all crises and challenges are God's way of speaking to us.

Every problem is an opportunity to grow and develop leaders and expands personal or corporate leadership capacity (read Acts 6:1–9).

27. Minister out of weakness like Paul the Apostle (2 Cor. 12:1–7).

When leaders minister out of brokenness and transparency, they gain the respect and trust of their followers and enable others to see the grace of God at work. When leaders brag about their spirituality or abilities, or preach condemning messages to their congregations, they discourage those struggling with their faith and walk.

28. Have a community-centric—not a church-centric—approach to ministry.

Most churches plan on how to bring people in the community into their church instead of planning how to send people from their church into their community!
I have found the most successful discipleship prepares people for life in the world, not just church life.

29. Honor older spiritual leaders who have influenced your life or region.

In 1999 our coalition honored twelve apostolic fathers in our city who had paved the way for younger ministries and churches. This was one of the highlights of my life. It broke open the heavens and imparted an incredible spirit of unity and cooperation in the New York City region!

30. Establish a strong intercessory ministry in your church for your family.

Satan tries to destroy the weekly prayer meeting more than any other meeting in a church!
Our weekly prayer meeting has become the spiritual epicenter of our church and the power behind getting our congregation and leadership behind our vision because they are exposed to God's heart for evangelism, discipleship, and city reaching.

Years ago we also established a prayer shield that includes armor-bearers who focus on praying for me and my family's needs. This has been a lifesaver. I encourage all those in senior pastoral leadership to have personal armor-bearers they can call upon in emergencies and that they can give monthly prayer requests to.

Bonus Lessons:

31. Raise up sons and daughters, not just church members.

32. Don't allow yourself to be in competition with other pastors and leaders in your region.

33. Don't try to copy another pastor's leadership gifts and church methodology.

There is only one "you." Also, each church has its own unique fingerprint that will leave an imprint on this world! Although we can learn much from other leaders and churches, we can never completely replicate anyone else because we all have different gifts, abilities, and callings.

34. Learn to enjoy life.

Cherish your key relationships, enjoy nature, and walk in the joy of the Lord! Those who always keep their feet on the gas quickly burn out their engines!

35. Have one or two high-level confidants.

Many pastors have no real friends, and even fewer have someone so close to them they can tell them anything without fear of betrayal. In a crisis, a general friendship is not enough. You need trusted confidants to bounce things off of to discern the will of God for your life.

36. Create a spirit of proprietorship in the organization.

Executive leaders need to discern the difference between those who have ownership and those who just show up to work. The key to success is to create an attitude of proprietorship in the church or organization so that a strong majority of members treat the organization as if they were the owners. Those who have the spirit of an employee don't really have a vested interest in the success or failure of the enterprise.

CHAPTER 8

Contrasting Kingdom Leaders and Church Leaders

Presently a revolution is taking place among those on the leading edge of change in the Evangelical Church. The result is a transition from a church mind-set to a kingdom mind-set in which the walls of church buildings are no longer able to contain the raw, creative energy of Christ-followers who are committed to preaching and applying the Gospel of the kingdom to all the world, including its systems and structures.

As political solutions and big government's attempts to heal our land fail miserably, more people will look to faith-based partnerships and churches to find solutions. Hence, the irrelevancy of old church patterns and traditions will become more noticeable in the decades to come.

Consequently, it behooves us to continue to study the contrasts between leading-edge kingdom practices and old, irrelevant religious church patterns that have failed to effectively evangelize and transform communities with the Gospel.

The following is a contrast between leaders with a kingdom mind-set and those with a church mind-set.

1. Kingdom leaders interpret Matthew 28:19–20 as referring to discipling all nations. Church leaders believe it only refers to all individual ethnic peoples.

The body of Christ is now rethinking the Great Commission scriptures of Mark 16:15 and Matthew 28:19–20. Instead of viewing them as commands to merely evangelize individual souls, now many are viewing the command in Mark 16 to "go into all the world and preach" as a command to apply the Gospel to both individual sinners and world systems. Matthew 28:19–20 is now regarded as the New Testament equivalent to the cultural mandate found in Genesis 1:28.

2. Kingdom leaders attempt to nurture and release world-class leaders who serve their communities.

Church leaders nurture only those who serve in Sunday ministry. Kingdom leaders understand that only 2 to 3 percent of those in their congregations are called to full-time church ministry. These leaders believe they are called to equip the saints for the work of the ministry, which, in the kingdom, includes marketplace vocational ministry, not only ecclesial ministry. With this view, there is room for everyone in the congregation to be set apart and trained as a minister of the Gospel.

3. Kingdom leaders understand and work with God's common grace.

Church leaders only understand and work with those who have experienced saving grace.
Kingdom leaders understand that God's grace has been poured out to all of humanity so the world can function normally. Romans 13:1–7 calls civic leaders God's ministers (*diakanos* or deacons). If God calls unredeemed leaders His ministers, then kingdom leaders know they can also partner with political and community leaders, even if they are not in full agreement when it comes to faith and core values.
Church leaders only work with those who are in full agreement with their core religious values, thus insulating themselves from the world around them.

4. Kingdom leaders have a biblical world view that encompasses all of life.

Church leaders have a semi–Gnostic Greek view of scripture that regards only spiritual things as important.

Kingdom leaders know that the earth is the Lord's and not the devil's (Psalm 24)! They know that the Word became flesh. Thus, the material world is also sacred and something to be cultivated (Gen. 2:15).

Church leaders are only concerned with spiritual things like prayer, healing, the gifts and fruit of the Spirit, etc. These spiritual things are only really effective if they are applied to our walk with God and its concomitant love of neighbor as salt and light.

5. Kingdom leaders are working toward a new Christendom.

Church leaders are only trying to produce individual Christians. Kingdom leaders desire to interweave the principles of God's word into every fabric of culture so every nation and city favors Christianity and bases civic laws on biblical precepts.

Church leaders are not overly concerned with politics and economics but with adding new converts who, without a biblical world view, will only perpetuate humanistic ungodly systems with their partial "spiritual" gospel.

6. Kingdom leaders teach the church to embrace their secular communities before they experience conversion.

Church leaders embrace people into their faith communities only after they experience salvation.

Kingdom leaders regard their cities and communities as gifts to the church and to the people who live in them. They embrace their communities in humility and send their members into their communities as servant leaders who will be the greatest problem solvers of the most challenging human needs.

Church leaders only embrace individuals in their communities after they have professed faith in Christ. Thus, they insulate and isolate themselves and their churches from the felt needs of their communities, yet are joyful as long as their churches are growing and their bills are paid.

7. Kingdom leaders turn the world upside down (Acts 17:1–7). Church leaders restructure their local churches.

In Acts 17 it was said, when the apostles came into a community, that "those who turned the world upside down have come here also."

Nowadays the typical church mind-set is only concerned with what happens within the four walls of the church building. Many of these churches could close down, and the local community boards, police stations, and political leaders would barely notice they were gone!

8. Kingdom leaders articulate Christ as Lord over every culture.

Church leaders preach Christ as only the head of the church. Kingdom leaders recognize Jesus's place as king of every secular king. This has vast cultural and political implications and pressures the church to engage the secular arena.

Those with a church mind-set only preach Christ as the head of the church and neglect Jesus's function as king over the unredeemed world!

9. Kingdom leaders shepherd whole communities.

Church leaders shepherd only their church congregations. Kingdom leaders understand they are called to communities, not only to local churches. Hence, they see themselves as chaplains and spiritual leaders of regions. Church leaders feel no responsibility to their communities because they feel committed only to those who attend their Sunday services.

10. Kingdom leaders attempt to exorcise demons out of ungodly social systems.

Church leaders only cast devils out of individual people. Kingdom leaders understand that Jesus came to redeem systemic sin, not just individual sin (read Colossians 1:20). Church leaders only feel called to deal with individual evil. Thus, they interpret passages such as Luke 4:18 as dealing with the individual poor and oppressed, neglecting the systemic reference from which it came. (Read Isaiah 61:1–4 to see that Luke 4:18 concerns redeeming and restoring desolate cities, not just individuals in need.)

11. Kingdom leaders pray for God's will to be done on earth as it is in heaven. Church leaders only pray for revival in their churches.

The Lord's Prayer (Luke 11) teaches us to pray that God's will would be done and His kingdom would come on earth. Thus, kingdom leaders have as their prayer focus the kingdom being manifest on the earth. Leaders with a church mind-set are content with only the signs of the kingdom (healing and deliverance of individuals as found in Matthew 12:28 and Hebrews 2:1–3) instead of striving for a manifestation of the kingdom in their cities that improves the quality of life politically and economically (Isa. 61:3–4).

12. Kingdom leaders believe for the Gospel to economically lift whole communities.

Church leaders merely believe for greater tithes and offerings to support their building projects and programs.

13. Kingdom leaders gravitate toward the complexities and challenges of cities.

Church leaders gravitate toward lives of isolation and inward focus. Before the Civil War, when the American church preached the kingdom message, the church was able to draft the founding documents of this great nation and start public schools and Ivy League universities, all for the purpose of placing godly leaders in society as the future presidents, governors, mayors, scientists, artists, writers, etc. The church took the lead in cultural reform.

But after the horrible experiences of the Civil War, the church lost hope in the kingdom being manifest on the earth and started to focus on the imminent return of Christ and the rapture. This resulted in American culture being lost to secularists in one generation!

This turning away from the kingdom message led to church leaders isolating themselves from the looming threats of biblical higher criticism, Marxism, Darwinism, the infiltration of non-WASP immigrants, Sigmund Freud and psychology, and the Industrial Revolution. The Industrial Revolution also placed many burdens upon the nuclear family, as men had to go into the cities to find work. Instead of engaging the culture and these challenges head on, the American church started looking for escape and changed its theology! The present move of God is finally bringing the church back onto the biblical footing of the kingdom message.

14. Kingdom leaders equip people for life. Church leaders equip people for church life.

Kingdom leaders inspire and equip the saints to serve in their cities as salt and light, to be like Daniel and Joseph who prospered and held significant leadership roles in the midst of pagan systems and kings. Church leaders train people to be good altar workers, ushers, Sunday school teachers, Sunday preachers, etc.

15. Kingdom leaders honor Jesus' dual role as Redeemer and Creator. Church leaders separate redemption from creation.

Kingdom leaders realize that the Jesus who died on the cross (John 3:16) for the sins of the world (John 1:29) is the same Jesus who created the world (John 1:3–4). When we apply the word of God to culture, we are embracing Jesus's ownership of the whole world. But when we preach the cross of Christ only for individual sinners and do not also apply it to the created order, we separate the redeemer from the creator!

16. Kingdom leaders are forward thinkers. Church leaders long for the past.

Kingdom leaders are excited about the future advance of Christendom in every facet of life and for every nation. They are excited over the increasing influence of Christ in culture. They train believers to replenish the earth by placing godly leaders in the realms of science, art, media, education, economics, and politics. The sky is the limit for them!

Those with a church mind-set long for the past, when life was much simpler and everyone in a community embraced the role of Christianity in culture. They do not like the vast complexities that social fragmentation has presented because it distracts from, and interferes with, their nice Sunday parish structures.

17. Kingdom leaders apply their faith to the earth.

Church leaders are focused on escaping the earth and making it to heaven. The Bible is essentially not a book about heaven. It is not concerned with another geographic location, whether spiritual or physical. It is mainly concerned with the person of Christ and His rule and dominion in the cosmos (read Ephesians 1:9–11). Because of this, the Bible is the most practical book about life on the earth that has ever been written! Kingdom leaders understand and embrace this reality.

Church leaders emphasize heaven since they have no real sense of purpose to give to the majority of their congregants who are not called into full-time church ministry.

18. Kingdom leaders envision the building of universities with theology serving as the "queen of the sciences."

Church leaders envision the establishment of church-centered Bible institutes that avoid liberal arts and the humanities.

19. Kingdom leaders are entrepreneurs.

Church leaders are stuck in maintenance mode, merely holding their ground until Jesus comes back or they make it to heaven!

20. Kingdom leaders pray for revival to bring people into the church and reformation to place believers as leaders in world systems.

Church leaders merely pray and believe for anointed Sunday services.

21. Kingdom leaders work for cultural transformation. Church leaders focus on waiting for the rapture.

Jesus told the church to occupy until He comes. Kingdom leaders are busy strategizing how they are going to start schools of government to train political candidates, start businesses to create wealth to expand the kingdom, and develop educational programs to break cycles of poverty for at-risk children.

Those with a church mind-set do not get involved in quality-of-life issues because their theology doesn't allow for it! They think it is like arranging the chairs on the *Titanic* because the world will soon end when the antichrist takes over!

22. Kingdom leaders train their children to walk in biblical dominion in society.

Church leaders' highest hope is that their children don't fall away from the faith! Kingdom leaders have dominion as the primary goal for their children. They don't teach their children to get secure jobs in big companies; they teach them to become the CEOs of Fortune 500 companies! They don't teach them how to fish but how to own a lake! They echo the words of Moses in Deuteronomy 28:10–13 that teach us that believers are called to be the head and not the tail, to be above and not beneath, to lend to many nations and not to borrow!

Church leaders take a defensive posture with their children by merely praying that they would not fall away from the faith. Even many who teach apologetics and biblical world view are stuck in the church mind-set because they are only teaching their children how to defend the faith instead of also how to advance the kingdom!

23. Kingdom leaders empower the poor to own the pond. Church leaders give the poor some fish.

Kingdom leaders understand how to break poverty mind-sets over people by equipping them to create their own wealth. Church leaders have an entitlement approach in which they merely feed the poor instead of equipping them to start their own businesses or to work in high-level positions that will enable them to be prosperous for the sake of the kingdom!

CHAPTER 9

Eight Power Principles for Transformational Leadership

The following are eight of the most important leadership principles I have learned as a senior leader over the past three decades. I have found that each of these leadership principles is vital to the success of any organization, whether it is faith based or not.

1. They continually cast a compelling vision.

The Bible teaches us that without a vision the people perish (Prov. 29). This means that people are like sheep and will scatter and lose focus if they are not continually motivated and guided as to the mission and purpose of the organization or church they belong to.

Every executive leader must be personally empowered and full of passion so he or she can continually remind the people of the vision and purpose of their existence. An organization without a compelling vision is going to lose momentum and membership. A leader without a compelling vision doesn't know why he or she is leading, which will result in his or her organization experiencing a lack of cohesion and power.

2. They set practical goals to attain their vision.

Having vision without practical goals to implement the vision is tantamount to merely having a dream that disappears once you wake up. Even if your vision was given to you supernaturally by the Lord, goals are necessary to take it from the mystical realm to the practical realm. For an effective goal, I like using the acronym SAM. Each goal should be
S—specific,
A—attainable,
M—measurable.

If a goal is too ambiguous, then it is no good. (For example, "this year our church will grow larger" is too ambiguous.) If a goal is too lofty and not attainable, then it is a pipe dream. (For example, "this year our church will grow by 50 percent," when it has never grown more than 5 percent in the past twenty years, is unrealistic.) If you do not revisit a goal to evaluate if you achieved the desired results, then it was not measured and is worthless.

Eventually, when the principles of SAM are not followed, the people in the organization become discouraged and believe that the vision of the leader is nothing more than rhetoric and good oratory, and they will cease following him or her.

3. They build strong, competent teams to perpetuate the vision.

Every leader needs to process the vision and mission of the church with a competent team that will have ownership over its fulfillment. When leaders merely give out direction and orders to their teams, then they are creating followers who can't think for themselves. Thus, as the organization grows, the leader will have more and more burdens upon his or her shoulders, which will eventually become a bottleneck.

However, when a leader builds a team around his or her strengths and weaknesses, he or she will have people around who will compensate for the gifts and abilities the leader doesn't have. A leader doesn't have to be the smartest or most capable person in the organization; his or her greatest job is to surround him- or herself with the smartest and most capable people and get them to work together to accomplish the task before them.

For example, macro directive leaders need micro operational people around them, as well as team builders, to fulfill their visions. When macro leaders don't have micro leaders, then there aren't proper systems or people in place to carry out their directives.

Finally, effective leaders are constantly encouraging and building the confidence of their teams, which counteracts all the negative things team members either think about themselves or the negative information they are bombarded with via media and relationships. One of the greatest things an effective leader does is build faith, confidence, and courage in his or her team so team members come to the place where they believe they can achieve great things!

4. They put first things first.

Effective leaders are continually grounding themselves in their core values of faith, family, and personal renewal. Those who are not grounded will either burn out or disqualify themselves because they will eventually fail to have integrity either within themselves or in their families.

In regards to their organizations, effective leaders have learned to put their finances and time toward empowering the people with the most potential, so they can bear the burden of the work and expand the capacity of the organization. They have also learned not to have transactional relationships that objectify people so that people only feel valuable if they are contributing to the success related to fulfilling their goals. When executive leaders treat people with dignity and respect, they will get more output than if they merely use and abuse people.

5. They constantly recruit emerging leaders.

The greatest baseball teams are the ones with the best farm systems that continually replenish the major league team with high-caliber players. Effective leaders are continually looking to recruit on to their team the best talent and most capable people who are also trustworthy.

One of the most important things I have done over the years is to meet at least once or twice a month with a primary leadership group and with an emerging leaders group of newer people who have the potential to lead in the next generation.

Organizations and leaders that do not recruit new leaders will be stuck with people who have already flatlined and will limit the ceiling of the vision. When you continually empower the next generation of leaders, it is easier to replace the team members who move on to other organizations or who disqualify themselves from remaining on the team.

6. They create a culture of accountability and trust.

There is an old saying "People won't do what you expect; they only do what you inspect." This is true. Many leaders are shocked when they find that what they say and teach is not being practiced or followed by the top leaders on their teams.

Ronald Reagan once said, in relation to how he dealt with the Soviet Union and its nuclear arms treaty with the United States, "Trust but verify." I have learned that if you don't hold people accountable, they will lose focus and not follow through on their tasks because of the many distractions that come their way. It is also good to require regular reports from your staff so that you can gauge the amount of work and productivity for each person.

Just as important as accountability is creating an atmosphere of trust with your top team members so there is an ability to share weaknesses, temptations, and even moral failure. A culture of trust will build greater capacity for love and teamwork and will empower all to move mountains and achieve great things!

7. They put the mission of the organization before their own personal agenda.

Many leaders who obtain power and affluence begin to think that the organization, ministry, or church they founded exists merely to serve their own personal needs. When leaders put their own personal needs and agendas before the mission and vision of their organizations, it creates a culture of self-centeredness that will eventually backfire because it will spread to all the secondary leaders, who will, in turn, poison the rest of the organization and its members. Self-focused entities do not have long shelf lives; if they do survive, they will not be effective.

Pastors should remember that God says very harsh things to shepherds who think the flock exists just to feed them and therefore merely feed themselves and do not minister to the flock of God (read Ezekiel 34 and Jeremiah 23).

8. They continually devise strategies to finance the vision.

As we read 2 Corinthians, chapters 8 and 9, we see that the apostle Paul devoted much of his time to fundraising for the vision of planting and establishing local churches.

It doesn't matter how much of a great speaker you are, how great your team is, and how talented you are; if you are not effective at fundraising, you will never be able to accomplish God-given goals and vision! Money and goals serve as the bridge between vision and reality.

CHAPTER 10

The Ten Commandments of Effective Spiritual Leadership

As someone who has been involved in some form of leadership and studied this subject for over thirty years, I have observed certain nonnegotiables in regards to what makes a person an effective leader. When it comes down to it, the most important elements of leadership are very simple. I have summarized these in ten fundamental commandments:

1. Thou shalt model what you preach.

The most powerful leaders are those who walk in private what they preach in public. Those leaders who personally live out the principles they expect from others maximize their influence and effectiveness as leaders.

2. Thou shalt develop leaders of leaders who can succeed you.

As soon as people become senior leaders, they need to start working themselves out of a job by empowering others to do what they are already doing. Those they pick should fulfill the qualifications Paul laid out in 2 Timothy 2:2. Consequently, when a person is able to do a job about 80 percent as well as the senior leader, the senior leader should delegate the job responsibility over to that person.

Those who don't have this attitude are never entrusted with more by God. That is because they limit their capacity by having too much responsibility and thus no leverage to go to the next level of assignment. Those who refuse to delegate will only produce followers who don't mind being limited in regards to leadership capacity because they don't like to think for themselves.

Conversely, the highest and hardest calling for senior leaders is to develop leaders who develop other leaders of leaders. Most leaders never develop anything more than followers. Leaders who develop leaders of other leaders are able to produce themselves in those who leave a legacy of developing leaders for many generations.

3. Thou shalt prioritize investing in people more than in programs and marketing

It is very tempting for a senior leader to put all his or her focus on implementing programs and marketing that will draw more people into the church or organization. Yet our first priority should always be pouring into people.

Those who spend most of their time administrating programs will never develop strong and deep disciples because the biblical discipleship process takes years and can only be done through personal interaction (both intense and informal).

4. Thou shalt communicate a divine, compelling vision worth following.

It doesn't matter how gifted a leader, a speaker, or a strategist you are. If you do not have a compelling vision from God, then other key leaders with potential will not follow you. Those with high leadership caps not only look at the leader they want to follow but also need to feel an emotional and divine tug regarding vision that speaks to their need for having a purpose (Acts 11:23).

5. Thou shalt learn to release others to help fulfill the vision.

Effective leaders are not lone rangers and do not try to accomplish a vision without a team. After you have invested in the lives of other potential leaders, the next priority is to discern where to place those you are mentoring. The key to high performance in an organization is for the leader to function like a sports coach and release each person to serve in a team in the areas best suited for his or her personality, gifts, and calling. The leader's vision must become a shared vision if it is to come to pass!

Some are more suited for dealing with administration and minutiae, and others are more suited for managing the big picture and people. Trying to put a big-picture person you are mentoring in an administrative role would not only hurt the organization's performance but could also crush that person's confidence and frustrate him or her.

6. Thou shalt hold yourself and your followers accountable.

All effective leaders allow for much freedom when it comes to ministry but have high standards of personal accountability when it comes to their marriages, families, and walk with God. Those who don't hold their leaders accountable in their ministries and home life could eventually lose the respect and focus of key people in their organization. In the worst-case scenario, people might begin doing their own things and developing their own visions, which will result in division.

7. Thou shalt practice Matthew 18:15–17.

Along with holding other leaders accountable, senior leaders need to insist that everyone who serves in the ministry with them must walk in the principles outlined by Jesus in Matthew 18. This has to do with walking in the light and in transparency with one another, without which people who work closely together will eventually develop bitterness and resentment and give themselves over to gossip, which could destroy the culture of an organization.

Senior leaders who are too afraid or passive to confront other people in their organizations will eventually self-destruct due to holding back bad feelings. This could lead to physical and emotional stress, marital failure, and deeply rooted resentments and bitterness.

8. Thou shalt affirm those who bear fruit and redeem those who fail.

Effective leaders learn to praise those who minister effectively and try to redeem those who are failing. If you quickly throw those who fail under the bus without trying to redeem them, then you will not develop the loyalty needed to have a strong core. This could result in a lot of turnover on your staff. When senior leaders successfully process people out of failure into success, the people are more likely be loyal to the senior leader for believing in them instead of dropping them. This kind of gratitude and loyalty will then spread and become part of the culture of the organization.

9. Thou shalt hold to high standards of excellence and integrity in service.

Along the lines of accountability, every leader needs to hold high standards both for his or her own life, ministry, and performance and for those who are serving along with him or her. Everyone and everything in the organization must have a spirit of excellence: the administration, communication, accountability systems, teaching, and physical appearance. If any of these areas becomes sloppy, it could bring down the quality and culture of the entire organization.

10. Thou shalt walk in wisdom and humility regarding the future.

All effective leaders must be able to see where their organizations need to go in the future based on demographic and cultural shifts. Leaders who do not change their approaches with changing times will eventually be bypassed by younger people in the next generation, who will gravitate toward those who speak their language and meet their needs.

In order to effectively change their approaches, leaders must always be humble enough to question themselves regarding their personal walk, their goals, their methods, and the way they are attempting to meet the needs of their communities. Those who are presumptuous and too arrogant to ask themselves these questions will eventually marginalize their influence.

CHAPTER 11

Eight Contrasts between Empowering and Disempowering Leadership Styles

Knowing how to nurture people so they reach their maximum leadership potential is as much psychological know-how as it is an art. There are ways leaders limit the creativity of others, and there are ways to get folks to reach new heights they haven't even dreamed about. The following are ways leaders can empower others to fulfill their potential:

1. Empowering leaders allow others to make mistakes.

Some leaders are more concerned with getting a job done correctly than about empowering people to learn how to do a job. When a leader only cares about getting the job done right, he or she won't truly delegate authority to others to perform a task. This is because these leaders view their workers merely as an extension of their arms and legs but not their brains, because they don't let their workers think for themselves. Often, they constantly correct those they give a task to perform as the job is being done.

On the other hand, empowering leaders often allow those who are assigned tasks to make mistakes and then gracefully critique those workers after each task is done.

2. Empowering leaders don't micromanage.

Micromanaging should only be done if a leader is working with a person who is completely untrained or unskilled at a particular task. This kind of working arrangement should only be temporary because a person should not be assigned a task he or she doesn't have the potential skill to perform. Once the transition to job proficiency is complete, the leader should allow the worker to perform tasks with only macro oversight.

Micromanaging breeds an atmosphere of distrust and tells the person given the task that the leader doesn't really believe in him or her. Habitual micromanagers usually don't have a clue when it comes to being empowering leaders.

3. Empowering leaders focus on the positive traits of others.

We all stumble in many ways. All of us usually drop the ball on assignments at least 10 percent of the time, depending on how much extra work we have. In addition, we are always going to make mistakes in a certain percentage of the tasks we perform. Also, one person will always do a job differently than the next person.

Consequently, a leader will always have the opportunity to point out things that a person didn't do correctly. Thus, the leader should attempt to focus most on what the person given the task did right and the results of the work performed. Of course, the exception to this is if someone totally messes up a task or doesn't follow the guidelines given to him or her.

When we focus on the positive contributions of others, we impart confidence to them and motivate them to continue to perform at a high level.

4. Empowering leaders give constructive criticism, not destructive criticism.

There should be regularly scheduled times after each major task is completed to review the work and assess whether objectives were met. This should be based on the criteria given before the task was attempted so there is an objective way to gauge whether or not the task was performed with excellence. Regular debriefing times like this allow workers to understand whether or not they are growing in the job and where they stand in regards to their employment.

It is not fair to tell people one year after they start a job that they are not performing well. By this time their jobs are already in jeopardy, and they haven't even been given a chance to improve because they had no feedback.

Those who desire to work with a spirit of excellence usually welcome consistent, constructive criticism. Of course, when a leader puts people down, calls them names, belittles them, or speaks in a condescending manner to them, he or she is dispensing criticism that can destroy, not build up, those working under him or her.

5. Empowering leaders give expected guidelines, goals, and outcomes.

Empowering leaders usually always give those working for them general guidelines for a job and the objectives of tasks, along with an idea of the end result they are looking for. This enables the person given the task to "run downfield with the ball" creatively without constantly looking over his or her shoulder wondering if he or she is still on the playing field.

Disempowering leaders merely give a person a task but have amorphous guidelines, goals, and objectives so that no one but the leader really knows if the job is being done right or wrong. When leaders do this, it is a sign that either they don't have real objectives for a task or that they are simply trying to keep exercising psychological control over their workers.

6. Empowering leaders connect people to their passions, gifts, and callings.

Empowering leaders always attempt to match people with jobs according to their gifts, passions, and abilities. Disempowering people don't consider these things and often are guilty of attempting to force a square peg into a round hole. Empowering leaders take pride in being able to help people soar like eagles to the highest heights imaginable, while disempowering leaders care more about getting tasks accomplished than releasing human potential. Empowering leaders also are sensitive and lead each person differently according to his or her experience, personality, and temperament.

7. Empowering leaders focus on inspiring people as opposed to forcing people to perform.

Empowering leaders cast vision so as to inspire their followers to perform great things, while disempowering leaders often get things done merely by giving orders and making demands on people. When you inspire people, they perform at a much greater level because they are allowed to make their own decisions to serve and have a greater amount of buy-in. In contrast, those merely following orders will do just enough to please the leader and usually don't tap much into their creative juices.

8. Empowering leaders engage in dialogue, while disempowering leaders dictate their desires and ideas.

Empowering leaders attempt to allow a flow of dialogue between themselves and their followers in work-related projects. These leaders understand the importance of receiving regular feedback from their subordinates so they will have a better understanding of how to go about accomplishing tasks. In contrast, leaders who disempower others don't usually engage in dialogue but merely dictate what and how they want a project done. Folks under this kind of leader eventually lose their motivation to think and just robotically follow orders because they know their opinions don't really matter. Dictating leaders usually don't multiply other leaders; they are merely retaining followers who have allowed their creativity to be capped.

CHAPTER 12

Nine Contrasts between People-Pleasing and Principle-Centered Leaders

The general axiom regarding leadership is this: if your greatest goal is to please people, become an entertainer; if you want to be a great leader, expect to have continual opposition.

Nine Traits of Crowd-Pleasing Leaders:

1. They care more about being sensitive than solidifying their team around vision.

There are times when you have to take people off your team because their laxity regarding commitment waters down the standard necessary to obtain the goals. Other times leaders have to let certain people go because their qualifications do not match their desire and passion. Faithfulness is not enough sometimes; ability plus faithfulness is the match needed to accomplish purpose. When a leader is making these necessary changes, feelings are sometimes hurt.

2. They become men pleasers rather than God pleasers.

Remember King Saul's response to the prophet Samuel when rebuked for not obeying the Lord (1 Sam. 15:19–24). Saul was removed from being the king of Israel because he cared more for the opinions of men than the favor of God. Truly, "the fear of man is a snare" (Prov. 29:25). Many elected officials tend to take public opinion polls and consult focus groups before they do anything of consequence. This may be necessary to gauge the attitude of the culture, but public opinion should never become the plumb line regarding ethical standards. We have too many politicians, not enough statesmen!

3. Their emotional state is dependent upon the affirmation they receive day-to-day.

Strong leaders are driven by the vision the Lord has given them, not by the daily conversations and affirmation of their staff, team, and those around them. Those driven by a need for affirmation usually have emotional highs and lows that go up and down like a yo-yo. They are always either very happy or very depressed depending upon other people's assessment of them.

4. They don't have clarity of mind and heart regarding the voice of the Lord.

Because they are always subconsciously caught between two opinions (discerning the voice of God and the will of the people), their spirit is muddled, and they become duplicitous. You can only serve one master. You cannot serve God if there are other gods in your life.

5. They don't communicate based on the full spectrum of truth.

They only either preach wishy-washy messages or communicate one-on-one in a way that is postured more to please the listener than to present the truth at hand.

6. They tend to avoid confrontation and value peace more than victory and truth.

Crowd-pleasing leaders will be one way with one person, then another way with another person. Their desire to be liked is so strong that all their relationships are duplicitous and never reflect core values and principles. Consequently, every person these leaders speak to thinks they agree with him or her, even those sitting on opposite poles conceptually.

7. They tend to run a very informal and lax organization.

They run a laissez-faire (anything goes) organization that often has very little administrative and organizational excellence. Often, they allow a culture of ease that lacks excellence with an unaccountable environment.

8. They tend to overpay their staff.

They pay to please rather than remit pay commensurate to the quality and skill of the employee. They reward staff based on personal affection rather than on job performance. This "good ol' boys' club" eventually goes out of business because of underachieving.

9. They are intimidated by principle-centered leaders.

People pleasers are generally intimidated by principle-centered leaders because they do not know how to manipulate them with flattery. People fear what they cannot control.

Nine Traits of Principle-Centered Leaders:

1. They lead based on principle, not on people.

The divine vision they have trumps the affirmation they receive from the people. Thus, they are not afraid to make decisions that displease their staff or some of the people they lead. They realize that people will respect them more if they hold to principle than if they vacillate based on people.

2. Their hearts and minds are focused on pleasing God first.

God-centered leaders are able to hear the voice of the Lord clearly. Their minds and hearts are not weighted down with the worry of pleasing every person around them.

3. They are secure in themselves because they receive their primary affirmation from the Lord.

Secure leaders know who they are and what they are called to do and focus on their primary assignments.

Insecure leaders are scattered because they are always saying yes to everyone and never have enough time to get tasks done correctly.

4. They hold up under duress while in the midst of those who oppose their vision.

If leaders were administered an emotional IQ test, the most common trait of great leaders would be their ability to handle an enormous amount of stress and their ability to problem solve.

Principle-centered leaders have the greatest strengths in these two areas because people who are doing the right thing have more perseverance and clarity of thought.

5. They have organizations built on integrity and truth.

Principle-centered leaders have the best chance of building multigenerational organizations because what is built upon truth will last the longest.

6. They are not afraid to confront others in love.

One of the most common reasons for stress is that most people bottle up their emotions because they are not willing to confront other people. Hence, they layer their anger, resentment, and pain with busyness and phony relationships that fail to get to the root of the issues.

The Bible commands us to confront one another, have transparent relationships, and keep short accounts (Matt. 18:15–18; 1 John 1:7).

7. They have stable personalities and are consistent.

Because their affirmation is from the Lord, principle-centered leaders are upbeat and filled with vision, purpose, and joy. They are living to please the Lord, not the mercurial emotions and desires of people. Those around these leaders know that, no matter what season it is, their leaders will always be consistent in their actions and goals.

8. They value truth and principle more than peace among their team.

They would rather lose a team member than compromise the vision or obedience to the Lord. (Of course, we are speaking about major issues, not minor things we are called to overlook in love.)

9. They understand that engendering respect is more important than engendering feelings of love.

Leaders are not called to be everyone's close associate or friend. A leader will go a lot further with the gas tank of great respect than that of love. Principled people will tend to follow a leader they greatly admire and respect more than a person they merely love. Respect is earned from years of having a good track record of accomplishments; love can come after just one deep conversation.

CHAPTER 13

Discerning Wolves, Sheep, and Horses in a Church or Organization

The Bible uses certain animals as metaphors to depict certain kinds of people in the kingdom. To be effective leaders, pastors and senior leaders of organizations need to discern at least three kinds of these animals among people in their organizations.

Although most people may have a mixture of all three animal traits at times in their lives, it is very possible that either the negative or positive traits of a person can suck him or her fully into either the dark side or the light of the Kingdom of God. It is inevitable that every growing organization or church will attract all three of these kinds of people simultaneously.

Following are some of the main characteristics of wolves, sheep, and horses as based on my observations during more than thirty years of ministry in the church and marketplace.

Wolves:

Wolves say yes outwardly to spiritual authority but say no in their hearts.

Wolves attempt to fool the shepherds among them by outwardly being agreeable to the vision, ministry, and responsibilities of the organization, but inwardly they have no intention of fully obeying spiritual authority. In the beginning they will either do the absolute minimum of what is required—or maybe even excel—but they do so merely to position themselves into a place of trust among the leadership so they can leverage more influence and fulfill their fleshly schemes.

Wolves have their own visions.
Senior leaders make mistakes when they think that division in their ranks only comes from gossip or

slander. There is more division in churches and organizations than most leaders realize because its covert operation is not based on slander but on hidden agendas. Any person who perpetuates his or her own vision within the overarching vision of a church or organization is in fact a divisive person and a wolf in sheep's clothing.

Wolves are not ministerially accountable and walk in the dark.

Any person or secondary leader who doesn't allow his or her overseer to see what kind of work he or she is doing, gets annoyed when asked for reports, shuns honest, open relationships and accountability, or obstructs usual communication systems is potentially a wolf in the making.

Wolves are not authentic because they attempt to look like sheep.

People who are not authentic within themselves are candidates for turning on others at any given time. If you are not true to yourself and to whom God made you, then you will not be true to other people. Wolves wear sheep's clothing because they attempt to fit into the overall scheme and structure of an organization or church. That is to say, they fit right into all of the cultural norms of their surroundings.

For example, if they are in a church, they will regularly attend church services and leadership meetings, pay their tithes, perform ministry tasks, and attempt to outwardly excel in spiritual disciplines more than anyone else. Most pastors are preaching every Sunday to a percentage of people who are wolves since they have no discernment, or because their church is too large for them to smoke the wolves out. Given time, wolves will attempt to position themselves in some way for more influence so, generally speaking, a senior leader will eventually find out who these people are.

Wolves position themselves to be close to those in power.

As stated in the previous point, wolves crave proximity to power. They will attempt to garner favor with the senior leader by acts of service, sacrifice, financial giving, and flattery of the leaders among them who are the most susceptible to false praise. For example, if the senior leader is not accessible enough, wolves will work to attach themselves to secondary leaders they perceive have influence with the senior leader. They do this to curry favor with the secondary leader to slowly build another infrastructure loyal to a subversive agenda instead of to the senior leader and the vision of the organization.

Wolves desire the perks of the organization without paying the price for the organization.

I have learned that those who really have sincere hearts will function in any capacity without a title or position, as long as they are properly stewarding their gifts. Since wolves don't want to pay the price over the long term, they position themselves to receive accolades, prestige, and a platform as quickly as possible—even over those who have paid the price for the organization for many years.

Senior leaders have to be wary of those who constantly crave positions, titles, and authority without proving themselves over the long haul.

Wolves camouflage their motives and actions with spirituality.

These people are not open regarding their personal flaws. Rather, they attempt to put up a veneer of superspirituality to fool others to the point that even the senior leader is not really spiritual in comparison to them. Their criticisms are not outwardly slanderous but consist of subtleties and innuendos that involve second-guessing senior leadership decisions or implying that the church isn't spiritual enough or that the senior leader doesn't really hear from God and doesn't really pray much, etc. Basically, wolves try to do anything that can successfully instill seeds of doubt about the senior leader in the minds of the people around them.

Wolves use and abuse people to accomplish their own agendas.
Although wolves come off as loving everyone around them, they are only using these people to gain influence and power. As soon as they have what they want from these naïve people, they eat them, spit them out, and move on to the next person who can deliver them the platform they desire.

Wolves can't be led but must be driven away by shepherds.
Some senior leaders attempt to rehabilitate every person who comes into their church or organization. This is a huge mistake! A wolf will always be a wolf, a sheep always a sheep, and a horse always a horse, no matter how much you fast and pray for them. Once a person is identified as a wolf, a shepherd should confer with other leaders for confirmation of this fact. Then the shepherd should monitor this person closely and not allow him or her any harmful leverage in the church.
In most cases, the senior leader can't just throw the wolf out. If the senior leader does this, then innocent people who have already been influenced by the wolf will get hurt as well. The senior leader has to wait until wolves reveal their true motives by "giving them enough rope to hang themselves." When it is manifest, they can be driven out!

Wolves attempt to destroy the shepherd as a way to consume the sheep.
By and large, wolves are in competition with the senior leader of an organization they are a part of, instead of serving as the leader's promoter and protector. The reason is that the shepherd (senior leader) has what

they crave: the most influence in the organization. Because of this, wolves will do everything in their power to tear down the shepherd so that the sheep are vulnerable to their wishes.

Wolves are not sons but bloodsuckers of the house.

Years ago, after we had gone through a very difficult time in our church, the Lord spoke through a member of our church, who said that God was going to give me "sons and daughters who would never betray me." Since that time I have built the leadership of our church with sons and daughters of the house, not with those merely desiring a position for their gifting to be displayed. This strategy has served our church well the past twenty years. I encourage all pastors to build key leadership with these criteria.

Wolves are not grateful for what the senior leader does or what the organization has to offer.

Instead, they are always complaining about their needs not being met. No matter how many times you aid a wolf, he or she will always crave more fresh meat to eat and blood to drink!

Sheep:

Sheep outwardly and inwardly attempt to follow their spiritual authority.

Sheep are those who say yes both outwardly and inwardly (in their hearts) to directives from those in spiritual authority over them. Sheep make up most of the congregation and will always gravitate toward a leader who is a legitimate shepherd that watches out for the best interests of the flock.

Sheep reflect the vision of the shepherd.

True sheep move in the general direction of the flock and reflect the vision of the shepherd and the organization. They don't care much about position or leadership. What they care about most is that their needs are met and that the organization has stability, especially in the midst of the storms of life.

Sheep desire to be accountable as long as they feel a place of safety.

Sheep will open up both their hearts and their wallets for the sake of a place of safety for them and their families. They want to be honest and open about their needs and hurts, and they greatly desire mature people they can trust who will listen to their cries for help and guide them toward the path of life.

Sheep run when they sense instability in a church or organization.

Sheep understand that while they are in pasture they will experience inclement weather, so they don't blame the shepherd for the storms of life or the attacks of the enemy on the organization. But one thing they will not tolerate: they will flee and run to another fold if they think the shepherd lacks integrity or is not a strong enough leader to continue to offer stability for the flock in the midst of the storm.

Sheep depend on shepherds to feed them and lead them.

Sheep will graze where they are fed. Sometimes when sheep leave a church or organization and go to another, it is because they are hungry and need green grass to be nourished. If the grass (preaching of the word) is stale or if the shepherd is not leading them besides still waters or helping them feel refreshed in their souls, they will eventually go where this is offered so they do not die of malnutrition. No matter how many responsibilities a senior leader has, he or she must always make sure the first order of business is to continually offer fresh, green grass (fresh, relevant *rhema* words from God) and pure water to the flock so they don't die of malnutrition or flee to other shepherds who will take care of them.

Sheep are vulnerable to wolves that prey on them at night.

Sheep cannot defend themselves, don't have much discernment, and may even wander off at night right into a pack of wolves. This is why a shepherd must continually identify where the wolves are and keep them away from the sheep. Sheep must also be closely connected to others in small group settings so they receive the proper oversight and care.

Sheep love and flock around true shepherds.

Sheep can always tell who a true shepherd is. One of the things I tell people who feel called to be pastors is that one of the proofs you are really called to be a pastor is that the sheep start gravitating toward you for comfort, nourishment, and advice. If you don't attract sheep, then, no matter how many years you had in seminary or how many prophecies you had spoken over your life, you are not yet ready to serve as a pastor.

Horses:

Horses are multipliers with unique leadership abilities in a church or organization.

Horses often are used as a metaphor for something stately and powerful. Probably less than 5 percent of people in any organization fit into this category. These folks are creative and multiply and develop other leaders, ministries, and programs. They are not the kind of people who like to be micromanaged. Like horses they need to have space to run and harness their energy.

Horses will say yes to spiritual authority once they understand the concept and buy into the agenda.

Horses are the kind of people who will be reluctant to get involved in something unless they fully understand the concepts involved. This is because they wisely manage their time and don't get involved in initiatives not suited to their gifting and mission.

Senior leaders need to recognize these kinds of leaders so they will not mistake their reticence for insubordination.

Horses will be transparent and personally accountable to those who train and release them to their potential.

Horses are the kind of leaders who will gravitate toward those who bring them to the next level. If senior leaders recognize a horse among them, they should prioritize pouring time into that person. Horses will usually hold themselves accountable and be transparent to a senior leader investing in them who has already developed a bond of trust with them.

Horses will reflect the vision if the visionary invests in them.

Horses will gladly perpetuate vision if they know the senior leader is creating capacity for them to grow in the organization and is willing to invest time nurturing them.

Horses will possess the vision if the visionary utilizes them to help fulfill it.

Often, sheep have ownership of an organization to the extent they are getting their needs met. On the other hand, once horses are loyal, they will exhibit a spirit of proprietorship. They are the kind of folks designed for battle and will be loyal and excel in their responsibilities—at times, even unto their own death!

Horses will carry the vision to the next level if the visionary rides upon their gifting and harnesses their abilities.

Horses, more than any other people in an organization, can carry numerous people on their backs while riding at light speed and promoting vision. To get an understanding of the growth capacity of a church or an organization, a senior leader merely needs to calculate the number of horses he or she employs on staff and as volunteers. Horses are the only ones in the organization with the innate potential to multiply other leaders and create ministry. Wise senior leaders will allow these (proven and tested) unique leaders to run swiftly and not be slowed down by overmanagement and insecurity (on the part of the senior leader).

Loyal horses will outpace and scare off the wolves.
Since horses have an amazing combination of speed and strength, they are the most capable in an organization to be released for battle in times of war. Wolves are intimidated by strong, loyal horses and will not mess with them and those in proximity to them.

Horses were born to race and will be bored with a slow pace.
Horses, like apostolic leaders, are used to moving, seeing, and working at light speed. (Sort of like in the movie *The Matrix*, when even bullets were moving slowly compared to the speed that Keanu Reeves's character moved.) Horses see so far ahead with concomitant speed that sometimes they assume everyone else is moving at the same pace.
Because of this, they can easily become bored. The senior leader must continually challenge horses by giving them the next big thing to conquer as soon as he or she sees a horse has mastered and established a particular assignment. Pastoral senior leaders cannot adequately oversee people such as these in the long-term; only accomplished apostolic leaders can stay ahead of horses in movement, strategy, and vision.

Horses crave accomplishment and significance, not titles or positions.
Horses are driven by accomplishment, not empty titles and positions. They don't need to be in the spotlight. They are usually alpha males (or alpha females) with a high type-D personality that is obsessed with solving problems, creating movement, and bringing

transformation and an improved quality of life to people, places, and things.

When people are vying for positions and titles, it is a good sign they are not horses but either confused sheep or wolves in the making.

Horses are potential successors to visionaries.

Horses are the only folks with the potential to take an already established apostolic organization to the next level of vision and destiny. Senior leaders who are transitioning out of their organization often make the mistake of choosing an administrator instead of a horse.

This is why apostolic movements usually settle for the status quo and concentrate on self-preservation in the second generation of their existence.

If you want an efficient organization, choose an administrator to lead it. But if you desire an effective organization, choose a proven, loyal horse with energy to create the movement necessary to expand the already established horizons for years to come.

CHAPTER 14

Seven Keys to Being an Effective Global Leader

Nowadays, with the flat-world reality of technology, it is easier than ever for key apostolic leaders to connect the world over. This incredible new ability to communicate should be done strategically and with wisdom, lest a leader fail because of a lack of focus. The following principles are important for all global leaders to follow.

1. Global leadership is exercised first at home.

Some leaders use world missions as a way of covering their ineffectiveness in their own regions. It is sometimes much easier for a church to send missionaries to Africa or China than to go across the street to minister to the African or Chinese families in its neighborhood. Acts 1:8 tells us to go to Jerusalem first and build a strong base like the original apostles did and then go to the ends of the earth.

One of the problems I have with some is that they teach principles on church growth or community transformation without having pioneered a model. True learning is doing and thinking, then writing what you have learned from your experience, not just thinking and writing.

2. Learn to deconstruct boundaries that keep people apart.

Effective global leaders have insight to understand different cultural contexts and become bridge builders that tear down walls between various ethnicities and nations. In this way the church models the Kingdom of God as a reconciled community of various groups of people under the lordship of Christ.

Regarding global leaders, I once heard Robert Calvert say their ministry must involve the following: listening without labeling (we size up people with our labels); agenda raising without antagonizing; being objective; not immediately criticizing others; not "busting" into someone else's territory; and collaborating without controlling.

3. Effective global leaders help indigenous leaders articulate and apply their unique assignments to their nations.

Sent ones (missionaries) who see the world only through their own culture or particular biases will be limited. They will attempt to clone and then franchise their ministries instead of helping indigenous leaders articulate their own unique callings and purpose, which are better suited to their cultural context. An example of this is when leaders try to export the exact strategy that worked in their local region to other churches in different contexts, in the same way McDonald's tries to hang its golden arches in every nation. For instance, I have seen disastrous effects occur (including church splits) when a pastor tries to replicate a particular kind of cell group method in his or her local church only because it has been successful in another country. Authentic global leaders help equip and release indigenous leaders to fulfill their unique visions without imposing their own visions upon them.

4. Effective global leaders serve the visions of key indigenous leaders.

When I go to other countries, I never go looking to plant churches or give apostolic covering to pastors; I point pastors and emerging leaders to the apostolic leaders already in their midst. I believe those who give apostolic oversight to pastors and churches in other countries insult those who have been called with a measure of authority in their own nations.

I believe indigenous leaders know and understand how to reach their own nations better than any outsider. For example, the Chinese church exploded in numbers, going from under one million believers in 1949 to over one hundred million today, all in less than sixty years *after* all of the missionaries were kicked out by the communists. This is because indigenous people know best how to apply the Gospel.

When I am in a foreign nation, I prefer to mentor or coach indigenous apostolic leaders and bishops instead of pastors. My greatest desire is to wash the feet of apostolic leaders already sent to their own nations and help them reach those nations. Of course, the exception to this would be if I went to a place where the Gospel has yet to be established (2 Cor. 10:13–16) or if there is no apostolic leadership available.

5. Effective global leaders network other global leaders together.

Networking is necessary and is a relational exercise that is less expensive than creating an organization. Networking usually results in the development of formal or informal society of leaders who commit to regularly keeping in touch to share information for mutual encouragement, for teaching, and for prayer toward the purpose of advancing the kingdom in their various spheres of influence.

6. Effective global leaders keep track of global trends.

It behooves Christian leaders on the world stage to read publications and websites such as the *International Herald Tribune, the Economist,* WorldNetDaily, the *New York Times,* the *Washington Post,* the *Wall Street Journal,* the Drudge Report, and other international information sources. Doing so will help them understand the times as the sons of Issachar (1 Chron. 12:32) and know how to prepare for global ministry. This will make leaders keener in their insight regarding the atmosphere in a certain region before they travel. For example, those going to China presently need to be sensitive to the political tension regarding Tibet, the pain regarding the devastation caused by the recent earthquake that buried alive thousands of schoolchildren, and the anxiety and pride the Chinese felt when hosting the 2008 Olympics. Thus, global leaders need to have a Bible in one hand and a newspaper in the other.

7. Effective global leaders learn how to balance family, local ministry, and global opportunity.

It has been said that the founder of World Vision was so busy meeting the needs of the world that he neglected his immediate family and lost one of his children to suicide. Global leaders need to have extra strong families and marriages so their base does not crack under the stress of being away from home for extended periods. Leaders also need to know how to properly time and space out international travel so they do not miss key local and family functions that emotionally connect them to their people at home. One time I had a guest minister speak at our church who bragged from the pulpit that he had missed going to his daughter's graduation so he could minister in various churches that week. Consequently, because of this and other things he said, I never had him back at our church.

Unless a leader's call is translocal, I tell leaders never to sacrifice their home base for extralocal ministry. Also, all travel should be restricted for senior leaders of new churches and ministries until sufficient leaders are available to minister in their places.

Finally, I believe God is calling the church to properly steward this incredible opportunity to unite global leaders for the sake of His kingdom. The early church was united and had evangelized much of the known world by the end of the first century—all without planes, trains, automobiles, cell phones, or computers. I pray nothing less will be done by His present-day church.

CHAPTER 15

Are You an Enabler or a Discipler?

The following is written in the context of a home group leader with his or her group members.

Traits of an Enabler:

1. You accommodate your message and approach to ministry based on the commitment level of your group rather than keeping biblical standards; your goal is to keep them happy and not make them uncomfortable.

2. You do not challenge your group members when they are not attending church, sharing their faith, tithing, giving offerings, living holy lives, and seeking first the Kingdom of God.

3. You do not integrate the ministry and vision of your local church in your group. (You should teach them about giving, pray for the vision of the church, and encourage them to be involved in the church as part of the group culture.)

4. You continually make excuses for those in your group when they are operating outside of God's will. For example, you excuse them when they are continually too busy to attend church on Sunday or when someone says something like "tithing isn't important because God knows my heart."

5. The noncommitted in the group feel comfortable around you. This is because you are (perhaps unintentionally) reinforcing their disobedient lifestyles due to either your own lack of conviction or passion in these dark areas or due to your desire and need for the group to like you outweighing your motivation to disagree, confront, and help conform them to the image

of Christ. (Of course, confrontation should always be done in love, grace, and mercy, but it must be done, or these folks will feel empowered in their disobedience rather than convicted.)

6. You sympathize (rather than empathize) with your group when they complain about their leaders or about how hard it is to fully surrender to God and give up the works of the flesh.

Traits of a True Discipler:

1. Your number one goal is to point people in your group to Jesus, not to you. Thus, your primary concern is getting your group to a right place in God's purposes rather than having them love you and agree with you on everything.

2. You don't hold back the whole counsel of God. You teach about uncomfortable things like keeping the Lord's Day first instead of family events (church attendance) and the giving of tithes and offerings. You do this because you love them so much you want God's blessing on their finances, so you attempt to get them financially committed and connected to the church.

3. You continually pray for the congregation, leadership, and vision of your local church in your group meetings so the group is inextricably connected to the life and vision of the church; group members don't feel comfortable substituting the group for the church.

4. You encourage them to volunteer to serve in the ministry of the church so they learn how to use their gifts and talents for the Lord.

5. You challenge and coach them regarding having a private devotional life with the Lord and a devotional life with their families.

6. You teach them, model for them, and exhort them to walk in forgiveness and build lasting covenant relationships with their immediate families and church family, not relationships based on a self-centered "I, me, my" existence but on putting others before themselves, as it says in Philippians 2:1–8.

7. You are empowering them to reproduce themselves. You teach them to live a victorious Christian life by winning souls, making disciples, and volunteering to serve others, instead of merely striving for selfish goals of having personal peace, having their needs met, and making it to heaven.

8. Your goal is to feed them meat, not milk. We are called to give babes in the Lord milk but are also called to eventually transition them to eat meat, as is commanded by Paul in 1 Corinthians 3:1–3 and Hebrews 5:12. Some of us are still treating those who have been saved for years as if they are new Christians!

Finally, when it comes to building covenant and making disciples, we are stewards of Christ and of His Gospel, the most privileged and most awesome responsibility in the world (1 Cor. 4:1–5)!

The call of the church is not to have a nonconfrontational social club (like a local pub) but a countercultural social army of disciples!

We are called to be on the frontlines of prayer, fasting, evangelism, discipleship, and societal transformation. But instead, much of the body of Christ has been on the frontlines of accommodating to the needs and desires of this consumption-obsessed culture.

Our call is not to make everyone happy but to exhort all to be purposeful! Although we are called to minister to the emotional needs of people, it must be on God's terms of discipleship and commitment, not on humanistic, self-centered terms that have no ultimate goal but self-preservation and pleasure.

It is important for those to whom we minister to love us, but they will not always like us in the process. Thus, it is more important to please God than men, as Paul said in his epistles (1 Thess. 2:4).

God is with us, as His Spirit will empower us if we are His witnesses (Acts 1:8) and not witnesses to ourselves and our own desires.

If you want to please all people, become an entertainer, not a leader!

CHAPTER 16

How to Change Culture by Mentoring Leaders

Although the book of Esther does not mention the name of God, there is perhaps no greater book that illustrates the ways of God and His sovereign hand! Those who read this book will quickly realize that Mordecai is one of the unsung heroes of the Bible. He used the following principles to save a whole race and transform a nation's laws and customs.

1. Mordecai raised up a capable leader who stood in the presence of a secular king (Esther 2:7–8).

One of the mistakes that many pastors make is to only raise up church leadership. We are also called to nurture marketplace leaders to "rule in the gates" to become the greatest servant leaders nations have ever seen!

2. Mordecai stayed close to the king's gate (Esther 2:21–23).

God is looking for Christ-followers He can trust to continually stay close to the gates of power. This will give us prophetic insight and discernment of the times. This will also give God's people the platform for the right opportunity to come along for kingdom influence.

3. Mordecai refused to compromise his faith while in the gates (Esther 3:1–5).

Often, men and women of God who get involved politically prostitute themselves for power and lose their salt, but not Mordecai! Like Daniel, he was able to immerse himself in secular culture without compromising his integrity.

4. Mordecai was aware of all the king's edicts (Esther 4:1–9).

Those serious about city and national transformation must have the scriptures in one hand and the newspapers in the other. They have to be people of the word and people of the world. Those serious about social transformation must also be willing to be in secular places of influence to garner the information needed as insiders to circumvent the enemy's schemes to destroy the work of God.

5. Mordecai knew when to access his insider's influence to change ungodly laws and systems (Esther 4:13–14, 8:3–6).

Astute leaders of influence know how and when to ask for favors from political leaders. They don't waste their time accessing power for every issue that arises. They only pull their "ace card" of access when it is an urgent matter that needs the assistance of a high-level official.

6. Mordecai was a man of fasting, prayer, and humility (Esther 4:1, 16).

I have found that the more I am involved in the so-called secular arena, the more prayer and fasting I need to stay spiritually sharp and strategic. Trying to win cultural battles merely through political means underestimates the nature of spiritual warfare that is won first in the spirit before victory is manifest in the natural realm (Eph. 6:10–13).

7. Mordecai waited on god to promote him (Esther 6:1–3).

Too many leaders in secular arenas fall into the trap of politicking or attempting to promote themselves instead of allowing God to be the one to exalt them (Ps. 75:6–7).

Those who are humble and wait on God are eventually honored even by their enemies (Esther 6:10–13).

8. Mordecai was positioned in power through the leader he nurtured (Esther 8:1–2).

Those who give themselves to pouring into and releasing leadership for the social realms of power will themselves be placed in positions of influence by the very people they poured into.

9. Mordecai rewrote ungodly laws (Esther 8:7–14).

Christian leaders shouldn't just preach against ungodly laws but be learned enough to help rewrite legislation to better reflect the Kingdom of God.

10. Mordecai's influence gave God's people a place of favor and power (Esther 8:17, 9:1–5).

People of God will use their influence in the gates of power to benefit the Kingdom of God in their region and not only themselves. Unfortunately, often people nurtured through the church forget where they came from once they attain positions of power and influence in politics. Their lust for power causes them to compromise the very values that enabled them to get influence to begin with!

CHAPTER 17

Contrasting the Discipleship Methods of Jesus and Jewish Rabbis

In order to understand the New Testament, it is vital for us to understand the cultural and religious background of Jesus and His disciples. With this in mind, it is helpful for us to understand the common discipleship method of the Jewish rabbis during Jesus's day, so we can gain a greater appreciation of His radical approach based on His claim of lordship.

On the surface there appears to be no essential difference between the discipleship methods of Jesus and that of the rabbis of His time. For example, both Jesus and the rabbis of His time had disciples or students who attached themselves to them.

However, a closer examination shows there are fundamental differences between these two approaches. The following shows these contrasts.

1. The *talmidim* (rabbis' disciples) chose their own teachers. Jesus chose His own disciples (John 15:16; Luke 9:57–62). Mark 5:18–19 shows how Jesus even rejected some who wanted to follow Him!

2. The talmidim chose a rabbi based on his knowledge of the Torah (the Old Testament scriptures) because the law was the center of Judaism. A rabbi only had authority commensurate to his knowledge of the Torah; the authority belonged to the Torah, not any individual rabbi.
In contrast, Jesus expected His disciples to renounce everything, not for the sake of the Torah but for His sake alone (Matt. 10:38). In the New Covenant, Jesus is the center of the universe, not the Torah (or the Bible). Read Colossians 1:17 and John 5:39–40. (Of course, the scriptures bear witness of Christ if read with an unveiled heart; read 2 Corinthians 3:15–18.)

3. In Judaism, being a disciple was only transitional—a means to an end—with the goal of becoming a rabbi. For the disciples of Jesus, discipleship was not a step toward a promising career; the following of Jesus was in itself the fulfillment of destiny (Rom. 8:29–30). There is no graduation or official degree that completes our discipleship process. It is an ongoing process that continues until our last breath in this life and beyond (Phil. 3:7–14; 2 Pet. 3:18).

4. Disciples of rabbis were only their students, nothing more. The disciples of Jesus were also His servants who committed themselves to obeying Him and suffering for His sake (Matt. 16:24–25; John 12:26).

5. The disciples of rabbis merely passed on their teachings. The disciples of Jesus were called to be with Him (Mark 3:14) and be His witnesses (Acts 1:8).

6. The disciples of rabbis were attempting to bring back the former glory of the nation of Israel. The disciples of Jesus were (and still are) the vanguard of the coming kingdom and await the second bodily return of King Jesus.

7. For the disciples of rabbinic Judaism, following the letter of the 613 laws, the traditions of the elders, and rabbinic interpretations of the Torah was of prime importance. But for Jesus, following these interpretations and pharisaic traditions was not as important as caring for the human soul. Read Mark 2:1–12 and 3:1–6.

8. The Jewish rabbis stressed separation from non-Jews and those who were unclean. Jesus taught that loving our neighbors is equal to loving God—regardless of whether a person is a Jew or not. Read Matthew 22:37–40 and Luke 10:30–37.

For more on the concepts presented in this essay, read
Transforming Mission by David J. Bosch, pages 36–39.

CHAPTER 18

Why Jesus Was Never in a Rush

As I ponder the life of Jesus, I notice that He was never in a rush as He walked among us, often taking time to minister to someone while He was on His way to minister to someone else (read Mark 5:21–43). This is foreign to many of us. That is because we attempt to use time-management methodologies instead of using life-management principles in which we plan for each day to center around a major agenda or category instead of mapping out each minute of the day.

The more focused a person is, the less rushed and harried he or she is because his or her specificity reduces the chances of engaging in unnecessary activity that eats up time. The general rule of thumb is this: the more unfocused activity a person is involved in, the less productivity, profit, and time he or she has for self-renewal, family, and meaningful ministry.

Here are twelve reasons why Jesus was never in a rush:

1. He knew His purpose.

In John 18:37 Jesus told Pilate that He is the king: "For this reason I have been born, and for this I have come into the world, to testify to the truth."

There was nothing ambiguous about Him; He knew the what and the why regarding His birth and purpose on the earth.

2. He knew His mission.

Luke 4:18–19 shows that Jesus had a vision regarding what He was supposed to do in ministry to fulfill His mission.

3. He had specific goals.

Luke 13:31–33 shows that He had a goal of where and when He was going to be in His travels.

4. He spent much time daily in prayer and only did what He saw His father do.

Read John 5:18–19 and Isaiah 50:4–7.

Harald Bredesen once said to a group of pastors, "If ministers would concentrate on only doing that which pleases the Lord and put that first, then everyone they are supposed to please will be pleased and ministers would not suffer burnout."

5. He was focused on people, not programs.

Matthew 9:36 shows us that Jesus was cognizant of the people and felt compassion for them. In Matthew 23:2–3, Jesus teaches against putting heavy burdens on people without helping them. In Matthew 23:23, Jesus put down leaders who emphasized the tithe without also emphasizing justice and mercy for people.

6. He concentrated on catching men and on developing leaders instead of on administrative duties.

Jesus only focused on what He and His twelve (and later His seventy) could accomplish. He wasn't bogged down with a lot of administration because He delegated to His disciples everything needed to release Him to concentrate on preaching, teaching, and training His disciples. Most churches would prosper if they would attempt to do away with every ministry that doesn't focus on evangelism and making disciples.

7. He knew where He came from and where He was going.

In John 8:14 Jesus told the Jews that His testimony was true because He knew where He came from and where He was going. Consequently, if people don't know where they came from (the genesis of life reveals the purpose and journey of life), then how are they going to know why they are here and where they are supposed to go?

8. He wasn't ego driven but was moved to minister by compassion (Mark 1:41–44).

Leaders who are driven instead of being led by the Lord are often competitive, insecure, and egocentric in regards to their ministries. They may work hard, but their low self-esteem drives them hard in their search for significance. Jesus was totally secure in His father; hence, He was never driven and never in a rush!

9. He knew when His ministry would be finished.

John 19:30 shows that Jesus knew when His ministry was over and said, "It is finished" before He gave up His spirit and died. Many people either don't end well, don't finish their purpose, or stay at a position long after they should have handed it off to a younger or more gifted leader.

10. He didn't minister outside of His assignment.

Mark 7:27 shows that Jesus wasn't going to minister to the Syrophenician woman because she wasn't under the covenant with God and didn't fit His target audience. In Matthew 10:5–6 He instructed His disciples not to go to any of the Gentiles or Samaritans; He wanted them to stay focused and purposeful. When you go outside of your God-given assignment, you step out of His grace and minister out of the flesh. This leads to ministerial burnout.

We can't be everyone's savior. We are not everyone's answer to prayer. You are not called to help every person you meet. (Sometimes Satan will even send people your way to wear you out!) Stay within your assignment, and you will prosper and be satisfied.

In our church I refuse to start a ministry (even if there is a great need) until God gives me a leader qualified to oversee it. The reason is that if I don't have a leader to manage a ministry, then either I or my office staff will have to manage the new ministry, which will put undue stress on us.

11. He didn't waste His time in meaningless conversation.

John 12:20–23 says Jesus never honored the request of the Greeks (who wanted to see Him) but ignored them and continued to enter the next phase of His ministry. I am not obligated to return everyone's phone call or e-mail or to meet with every person who wants to meet with me. I can't satisfy everyone's agenda for my life! I am only obligated to please the Lord and do what I see my father command me to do.

12. He operated out of His inner circle and delegated to them the ministry of helps that released Him to focus on preaching, teaching, praying, and accomplishing His purpose.

He had His three, His twelve, and His seventy minister to Him and for Him. The Gospel accounts show that it was His disciples who shopped for food (John 4:8, 27, 31), which released Him to minister to a woman in Samaria. Also, it was His disciples who arranged for the multitudes to sit down so He could feed them (John 6:10); Peter and John were told to prepare the upper room for Jesus to conduct the famous Last Supper (Luke 22:8–13); Jesus was asleep on a boat while His disciples took Him to His next destination (Mark 4:35–41). Thus, those He was training functioned in the ministry of helps to release Him to focus on preaching and making disciples.

CHAPTER 19

Twenty Different Kinds of Pastors

Having been involved in some capacity with pastors for over thirty years, I have come up with some personal observations regarding the different kinds of pastors I have either worked with or ministered to.

Since all of us (including pastors) have broken places in our lives, we can all struggle with and identify with some of the following categories. However, in this essay each category represents a lifestyle or habit pattern of pastors, not an occasional struggle.

My objective in this essay is to help pastors and leaders become self-aware and allow the Lord to deal with those broken places, as well as to help readers understand their strengths and weaknesses. These categories should also be applied as much as possible to any person or leader, lest folks in churches become judgmental of their pastors.

1. The Emotionally Sick Pastor

Many people have reported over the years that a large percentage of pastors feel depressed on Monday mornings, whether due to fatigue, lack of attendance on Sunday, low offerings, or other disappointing things related to their Sunday services. The incidence of depression among pastors is probably anywhere from 35 to 40 percent. Emotional health is usually not a priority for many pastors because, in their minds, their heavy workload doesn't give them a lot of time for self-renewal and introspection.

2. The Driven Pastor

Driven pastors are trying to prove something to themselves or to others. Ministry does not come out of a pure heart as unto the Lord but is related to an innate need for success. Hence, these pastors often push their congregations to finance building projects and other endeavors that are subconsciously motivated to help inflate their own sense of self-worth. This results in them attempting to do things the Lord never led them to undertake, which causes them to operate outside the grace and power of the Spirit.

These kinds of pastors not only continually drive themselves but their congregations to accomplish great things. Often they are also driven to excel beyond any other pastor in their community because their identities are wrapped up in being the most successful pastor rather than being anchored in Christ.

Of course, many of these pastors eventually burn out emotionally because they are operating on their own gifts and abilities instead of through God's leading.

3. The Fleshly Pastor

This is a person who never fully dealt with his or her issues of the flesh before entering the ministry. Hence, this type of pastor begins to fall into a lifestyle of sin as a coping mechanism to deal with stress and emotional pain. The more successful he or she is, the more temptation this pastor will have to deal with, since the more influence he or she has, the more stress and challenges he or she will experience.

Also, the more popularity these pastors have, the more opportunity they will have to engage in immoral behavior due to the mutual carnal desires between themselves and congregants enamored with them who are also trying to medicate their stress. This is why it is extremely important that people do not enter full-time church ministry as pastors until they have allowed the Lord to work inward holiness and spiritual maturity in their lives.

4. The Faddish Pastor

This kind of pastor is always attending conferences, reading books, and talking to successful pastors, trying to discover the next new thing God is doing. Consequently, he or she is always changing either the vision of the church or implementing church growth strategies according to the latest fads. These are unstable pastors who are unsure of themselves, their own walk with God, and their ability to hear from God.

They will also have a lot of turnover in church leadership because many of their key leaders will get tired of going from one thing to another and will look for a more stable church. These kinds of pastors really need to focus on universal, transhistorical and transcultural biblical principles of local church practice and mission and not try to copy every other successful model they see.

5. The Angry Pastor

This kind of pastor has unresolved anger, bitterness, and unforgiveness from past wounds that are either self-inflicted or the result of real betrayal. Instead of taking responsibility for their own failures, these pastors justify their lack of success by continually shifting blame toward others. Often their sermons are filled with angry denunciations about sin, different behavioral issues, and even specific people. Instead of ministering grace and faith in the power of the Spirit, they are ministering guilt and condemnation. They are always fighting something and someone and always seem to be a victim of satanic plots or people who are against them.

They also tend to blackball those who leave their churches and speak badly about anyone who doesn't agree with them.

6. The Superstar Pastor

These kinds of pastors always have an entourage surrounding them, are hard for individuals in the congregation to access, always wear the most expensive clothes, drive the best cars, demand huge honorariums to speak in other churches, and are generally superficial in relationships. They speak as if they have the most important ministries in the world and as if they are the most important men or women of God in the world! In their sermons they emphasize passages that illustrate how the anointing comes by serving the man of God (for example, Elisha and Elijah) but neglect passages in which Jesus speaks about not coming to be served but to serve (Matthew 20:28). Protocols related to honoring the pastor (or bishop or apostle, etc.) have to be strictly followed (legalistically) rather than having folks honor spiritual authority from the heart as unto the Lord. They may talk and preach about humility, but their lifestyle contradicts what they say.

7. The Professional Pastor

This kind of pastor has no real passion for the Lord or His people but views his or her pastoral ministry as a mere job or profession. He or she clocks in and clocks out and will move from one congregation to another, depending upon who can pay the highest salary or provide the best benefits. These pastors are the "hirelings" Jesus spoke about (John 10), who run when the wolves come to devour the sheep because they are not true shepherds but mere professionals. Those who look at being a pastor as merely a business or a profession instead of as a holy calling fit this category.

(Of course, by this point I do not mean that a pastor should not make a decent salary or be professional in how he or she conducts business. I am referring to the motivation, not the method, in this particular point.)

8. The Compromising Pastor

This kind of pastor will only preach popular messages that ruffle no one's feathers. These pastors will attempt to draw crowds, make people feel good, never preach anything negative, and go with the cultural flow and avoid controversial issues like abortion and biblical marriage. They will also placate their top tithers and give them positions of honor they do not deserve. These are the kind spoken of in the Gospel of John (12:42–43), who love the praises of men more than they love the praises of God. Compromise and the fear of man are also what caused the downfall of King Saul (1 Sam. 15).

9. The Legalistic Pastor

This kind of pastor puts all sorts of man-made rules, traditions, and regulations upon his or her congregation. Since these pastors have no real revelation of grace and lack a deep relationship with God, they have unreasonable standards and place burdens on men's shoulders they are unwilling to lend a hand to help lift. These pastors are confused and mix biblical commands with man-made tradition and place the latter on the same level as the former (read Mark 7:9–13).

10. The Progressive Pastor

A progressive pastor is always on the cutting edge of culture, technology, and new things happening in the church. While this is often a good thing, sometimes this kind of pastor does away with the old for the sake of the new, even when the old works best (whether it is replacing old leaders with new ones, following certain church practices, or changing structures of worship services, etc.). These pastors need older, more seasoned leaders speaking into their lives so they do not make unnecessary changes that will hurt more than help their congregations in the long run.

11. The Traditional Pastor

The opposite of the progressive pastor, this kind of pastor is a protector and maintainer of the old ways of doing things, whether they are effective today or not. The traditional pastor's love for tradition exceeds his or her love for souls and actually hinders him or her from hearing a fresh word from the Lord. Oftentimes, these pastors lead dying churches that are answering questions no one is asking anymore!

12. The Isolated Pastor

Isolated pastors have no deep relationships, try to work out every situation on their own, and are very lonely, all because of a lack of trust in their hearts toward other people. They do not work well with other church leaders and have only superficial accountability with their overseers. Since they lack the proper relational accountability and input, they tend to make decisions without seeing the full picture, which results in unwise decision-making.

13. The Independent Pastor

This is the alpha leader who thinks he or she has the best ideas and the most knowledge; is not open to having oversight and peer-based accountability; and is not a functional part of an association, network, or denomination. Not only is this kind of pastor independent, but his or her congregation functions independently as well, even if the church belongs (in name) to a denomination. These pastors lack the knowledge of the New Testament model of one-church/one-city, as we see in the epistles and in Revelation chapters 2 and 3.

14. The Seasoned/Balanced Pastor

This kind of pastor is balanced and mature, doesn't neglect his or her walk with God or his or her family, and is anchored in the Lord regarding his or her identity. These pastors minister out of the overflow of their walk with the Lord because their cups overflow! They have strong, transparent, and accountable relationships with their secondary leaders, peers, and overseers. They are not using ministry to prove anything to themselves; thus, they do not compromise the gospel they preach nor do they need ministry to feel good about themselves. They are ministers, not performers or professionals, and God can trust them with the sheep because they long to present every person mature in Christ.

15. The Mystical Pastor

This kind of pastor always says he or she is "hearing from God" and "thus saith the Lord." Many in this category also have frequent spiritual visions and dreams. They usually have an allegorical or mystical approach to biblical interpretation and don't usually exegete scripture with the intent of discovering the original intent of the biblical authors. Pastors in this camp emphasize certain kinds of prayer, worship, and spiritual ministry but have a difficult time connecting the dots and applying the Bible in a practical way in life and ministry

16. The Soulish Pastor

The soulish pastor is the opposite of the mystical pastor; he or she depends heavily on his or her intellect, rarely believes he or she hears from God in the Spirit, and generally thinks God only speaks to him or her through the scriptures. Soulish pastors usually have a very weak prayer life, are very analytical and doctrinal in their approach to preaching, and are afraid of spontaneity and unplanned moves of the Holy Spirit.

They usually oversee a church that emphasizes the word but has challenges with corporate and personal prayer participation.

These pastors also tend to split hairs over doctrine and often have a critical spirit of the charismatic movement and preachers who don't agree with them theologically.

17. The Caretaker Pastor

This kind of pastor builds a strong relational church, loves being with the sheep, and has an extensive counseling ministry. The congregations of these pastors are inwardly focused rather than outwardly focused, and they usually have smaller congregations because they like to minister in a church where they know every person's name. Thus, they do not really desire exponential growth, although they will receive it, if it happens to come. Their greatest weakness is a lack of soul winning and community outreach to the unchurched.

18. The Evangelist Pastor

The evangelist pastor is the opposite of the caretaker pastor because he or she is outwardly focused. These pastors have a gift of gathering large crowds and emphasize soul winning more than shepherding and discipleship. Their preaching is usually very powerful but is centered on the basics of the Gospel message of love, hope, healing, deliverance, justification by faith, and the eternity to come. The content of their messages is very basic, they are great storytellers, and they win a lot of people to Christ. But their preaching doesn't feed more mature Christians, who will tire of these messages after a few years, since their messages are not deep and not meant to feed mature saints. Instead, their messages are designed to win the lost and encourage faith in the congregation.

19. The Prophetic Pastor

The prophetic pastor usually has very deep messages, is strong on commitment, tends to have longer worship services, and spends a lot of personal time seeking God for vision and direction. He or she has high quality and high content services with a strong presence of God and does not hesitate to preach uncompromising messages that may offend some in attendance.

20. The Apostolic Pastor

Apostolic pastors are not generally good caretakers; are concerned with big-picture items regarding reaching their communities, raising up leaders, planting other church campuses, and expanding their facilities; and rarely get involved with counseling church members. Their churches have good systems, strong government, and stability combined with a good balance of outreach and in-reach. They need the ministry of the prophet to come in regularly to make sure the fire and passion of God is imparted to the congregation.

Finally, there are many more categories and subcategories of pastors I can probably think of, but these are some of the main ones I have observed. May the Lord use these categories to make us more self-aware in our leadership so we can continue to grapple with life's issues and grow into the mature leaders our churches and communities need.

CHAPTER 20

Eight Keys for Personal Mastery

God has given us inherent natural laws and spiritual laws that we can put into practice to gain mastery over the flesh, to excel, and to maximize our potential as human beings. Nonbelievers can also tap into some of these laws and excel in some areas of their lives because of the common grace that God extends to all.

The following are some of these principles that all leaders need to learn to walk in.

1. Have a positive attitude (Phil. 4:8).

The Bible commands us to only think of things that are good, pure, noble, and of a good report.
It is not just a matter of feeling good after you pray; it's a matter of always keeping a positive attitude.
It's never what a person does to you that matters; it's what you do to yourself with your thoughts that matters. Many of us allow hurtful words to continue to influence us and determine our future.

2. Visualize your successful future (Heb. 12:1–2).
Jesus endured the cross because He saw the joy set before Him. Don't let your present circumstances determine your future (Rom. 4:17–19).
Don't keep dwelling on your hurts, failures, or people who have let you down. Don't let these people continue to destroy you! Focus on all the potential, gifts, abilities, and power of God available to you as you believe in Him for victory.

3. Be consistent with short-term goals that are easily reachable.

When I started playing the guitar again (after laying it down for almost ten years), I didn't even know how to strum a chord anymore! I got back mastery of the instrument by practicing scales five or ten minutes per day several days per week. I didn't attempt to play seven hours per day seven days a week like I did as a teenager. Then I would have been discouraged and never started again. Start with small steps, and be consistent. It is amazing how effective consistency is! Even a commitment to a small amount of reading, praying, and practicing, if done consistently throughout the day in small amounts, will transform your life!

It has been said that if you read on one subject just one hour per day for three years, you will become an expert in that genre of knowledge!

4. Invest your time in your short- and long-term goals.

You would be shocked at how much time the average person wastes every day.

Every highly skilled person has the same twenty-four hours each day that the rest of the population has. If we would wisely plan how we are going to spend our time and invest it in something significant instead of watching television and videos, playing online poker, etc., then we would be able to accomplish great things! Every time you say yes to one thing, you are saying no to something else. If you want to live a life of leisure, you will never reach your full potential.

Even when I was working secular jobs in a camera store, in a restaurant, and as a security guard, I kept a small Bible in my pocket and read one book of the New Testament each day. During every five-minute break, I would study. During my lunch break, I would carve out time to study, and every day I was able to squeeze out thirty to sixty minutes of study per day, which made a huge difference!

5. Harness your passion toward things that will feed your primary purpose, not your hobbies.

Just because you have a passion for something doesn't mean you are called to focus on that. For example, I love to ski, play Ping-Pong and chess, and do physical exercise, but that doesn't mean I should engage in these activities several hours every day.
I also have a passion to study, mentor, and create communities that create a movement. Since these are all part of my primary purpose, I have devoted most of my time every day to thinking about how to excel in each of these areas.

6. Remain focused on one thing at a time.

When you are with your family, be present with them and not your work. When you are at work, be present there and not on a hobby. For example, when you are at work, don't surf the web or go on Facebook and allow distractions. This will stop you from excelling at your job and compromise your productivity. Give all your focus to what you are responsible for, when you are responsible to accomplish it!
James 1:8 states that "a double-minded man is unstable in all his ways."

7. Never compromise your core purpose, vision, and mission.

Purpose answers the question "why?"
Vision answers the question "how?"
Mission answers the question "what?"
The enemy of what's best is what's good.
I have a lot of opportunities on how to spend my time. I have to figure out whether or not an opportunity fits my mission (what I am supposed to focus on), and, if it does fit my mission, whether I have the time to give to do it with excellence.

8. Keep a healthy balance in life.

If you are not balanced, then your mastery in a particular area will suffer. For example, God made the human body so that its health is dependent upon every area being healthy and functioning correctly. A masseuse ministers to the muscles in the body; a therapist, to the joints in the body; and a chiropractor, to the nervous system in the body. When any of these systems are out of whack, your body, soul, and spirit can be negatively affected. A dentist understands that the hygiene of the mouth actually determines the health of the heart. Thus, a specialist in any medical or health field can claim that his or her field is the most important because each area of the body can be shown to affect the rest of the body.

That being said, I am called to be faithful, consistent, and excellent in every responsibility that is in front of me, whether it is my primary passion or not. (I have to pitch in to help the church, my family, and others in ways that may not necessarily fit my gift mix and passion. This is a test of faithfulness that develops character. If I can't be faithful in these kinds of responsibilities, then I am not balanced, and God cannot trust me with things having to do with my passion. The greatest in the kingdom is the person who doesn't think of him- or herself but functions as a servant.)

We are all called to live lives that put the Kingdom of God first in regards to family, vocation, and personal renewal. Life is a constant battle to keep a good balance in the shifting sands of life and circumstances. For example, I may give my whole life and focus to creating wealth and become very successful at it. But while I may gain mastery in the area of business, if I lose my health, family, or connection with God, it is not true success! Balance means I am working hard, playing hard, getting enough sleep, eating correctly, seeking God privately and corporately, and hearing what the Spirit is saying to the church so my contribution to our corporate destiny can be realized.

CHAPTER 21

What I Read and Why

Since I am called to teach and preach on the Kingdom of God, I have placed upon myself a very demanding reading regimen so I will have a biblical world view for every major arena of life. This means I cannot concentrate on only one area of study. For example, as much as I love reading history, I cannot only focus on that area because I would then be unbalanced in other areas. Hence, I have a continual diet of study that includes various areas of discipline.

Scripture teaches us to take every thought captive by the knowledge of Christ (2 Cor. 10:3–5). As this New Year approaches, I have an even greater hunger in my heart to study the word of God and books on other subjects that will better enable me to be a minister of the Gospel of Christ. The purpose of this essay is to encourage myself and other leaders and ministers of the Gospel to live a life of study and devotion that will be far greater than anything we have ever undertaken in the past!

I have a goal to study the following areas, with at least one scriptural verse to support doing so:

1. History, because I want to understand the present and be adequately prepared for the future (Prov. 22:3; Eccles. 1:9)

I study world history to see the hand of God on the nations; I study American history to better understand how and why our nation is in its present condition; I study church history because Jesus has been building, and the Holy Spirit has been teaching His church for over two thousand years, so I want to learn what they have been doing with the saints during this time.

2. Theology, because I want to continually grow in the knowledge of God (2 Pet. 3:18)

In past centuries, theology or divinity, as taught in Ivy League schools like Harvard and Yale, was called the queen of the sciences, and all other subjects evolved around it and could not be understood or placed properly without it.

3. Economics, so I can effectively steward my finances for the glory of God (Deut.8:18)

4. Apologetics (the defense of the faith), so I can be ready to give a reason for the hope that I have in Christ (1 Pet. 3:15; Jude 3)

5. Current events, so I can apply the Bible to contemporary life and culture and be relevant as the salt of the earth and the light of the world (1 Chron. 12:32)

6. Eschatology (the doctrine of last things), so I can learn how to live my life today (Eph. 1:9–11)

Truly, our eschatology always determines our protology (our understanding of God's purposes for humanity)!

7. Biographies, so I can model my life after the ways of good people (Prov. 2:20)

8. Philosophy, so I might know how to answer those taken captive by empty philosophy (Col. 2:8)

9. Leadership and management, so I can more effectively grow organizations I manage and nurture world-class leaders for the next generation (2 Tim. 2:2)

10. Science, so I can more adequately declare the glory of God (Ps. 19; Rom. 1:20–21)

11. Nutrition, so I can glorify God in my body by practicing preventive holistic health (1 Cor. 3:16–17)

12. Literature, so I can relate to books from the past and present that have framed societal thinking (Dan. 1:17)

13. Poetry and art, so I can relate the Gospel through metaphor, beauty, and subtlety (Prov. 11:30; 1 Cor. 9:19–23)

14. Music, so I can connect emotionally with nonbelievers I have befriended

15. The writings of the mystics (for example, A. W. Tozer) so I can obey the greatest commandment and grow in my love and devotion to Christ (Matt. 22:37–40)

16. Emotional health, so I can live a balanced life and mature in self-awareness (1 Thess. 5:13)

17. Marriage and family, so I can love my wife as Christ loves the church (Eph. 5:22–6:4)

18. Urban missiology, so I can learn how other urban practitioners are making a difference in their communities (read the book of Nehemiah)

19. Action research, so I can learn effective ways of proving theories, and so I can become a contemplative practitioner (Luke 9:10)

20. Motivation and self-help, so I can sharpen my life skills and obtain personal mastery in areas related to my calling (Gen. 1:26; 1 Cor. 9:26–27)

21. Growing trends and statistics, so I can properly analyze where the church and culture are heading based on God's sovereign hand (Dan. 2:20–22)

22. Christian psychology, so I am better equipped to minister to the emotional needs of others (Luke 4:18)

23. Sociology and anthropology, so I can learn case studies of human behavior and better understand human nature (John 2:24–25)

24. Biblical and contemporary law, so I can apply God's moral and civil law to public policy

25. Most importantly, the Bible, which alone has, in seed form, the universal principles of every discipline mentioned above and beyond, so I can live a wise life, be equipped for every good work, discern between my emotions and my spirit, and live a prosperous life, growing in faith that comes by continually hearing the *rhema* word of the Lord (2 Tim. 3:15–16; Heb. 4:12; Josh. 1:8; Ps. 1; Rom. 10:17)

CHAPTER 22

Good Cop, Bad Cop Leadership Syndrome

In my thirty-plus-year journey as a leader, I have sometimes noticed that certain associate leaders have a hard time backing up some of the protocols set in place by their senior leaders. This often results in the associate leader playing the role of the "good cop," making the senior leader the "bad cop"!

For example, a senior leader might reprimand a staff person for being habitually late, while an associate leader might be sympathetic and look the other way or even agree with the staff person's reasons for being late. In this situation, the associate leader is making the senior leader look like an uncaring, bad person.

This kind of "good cop, bad cop" syndrome is at worst done intentionally by an associate leader to win away the hearts of the people from the senior leader in the same way that Absalom stole the hearts of Israel away from his father, King David (2 Sam. 15:1–12).

At best, this associate leader is merely afraid of confrontation and becomes an enabler of bad habits that lower the performance standard for the entire organization. Even in this latter scenario, the senior leader is seriously undermined by the nonconfrontational approach of the associate leader.

Senior leaders need to be aware of associates who would purposely leverage themselves in certain situations as the "good cops." Also, senior leaders need to have associates who have the loyalty to publicly stand behind their decisions and protocols—whether they agree or not. Associate leaders who continually undermine executive decisions (whether intentionally or unintentionally) need to be corrected and, if necessary, removed!

CHAPTER 23

Ten Principles for Senior Leadership Succession

Unfortunately, leadership succession is usually one of the messiest things that ever happens in a local church! Most of the time, there is no real plan. If there is a plan, usually it is not well thought-out, and a person is prematurely installed as a senior leader and falls on his or her face.

The following are principles I have learned through experience regarding transitioning people properly into senior leadership positions:

First, we need to make sure a person has been functioning in a senior leadership capacity before hands are laid upon him or her and he or she ever receives the title. Pastors make a huge mistake when they commission someone untested and unproven to take their place as senior leader. Many churches actually choose a person to be the senior pastor based on hearing him or her preach on a Sunday! (I wish the only thing a senior pastor had to do was preach good sermons. Preaching is the easiest thing I do as a pastor!) Never give a person a title before a function. Titles don't make the minister; they merely affirm what the minister has already been walking in.

Second, any potential senior leader should be a spiritual son with the same DNA as the senior leader, so that the vision can be perpetuated. I have seen disastrous situations where churches of multiple thousands were reduced to only several hundred in just a few short years because they put in the wrong person (with a different vision) to replace the senior pastor! The most capable person to take the place of a senior pastor is a spiritual son who already has the vision and the DNA of the church imprinted in his or her soul, so the person can organically lead the church according to the divine pattern God gave him or her.

Third, the candidate for senior leadership should have already gained the respect and affirmation of the congregation. It doesn't really matter what candidates think of themselves, and ultimately it doesn't even matter what the senior pastor thinks of them. The greatest test to determine the legitimacy of successors is to see how the congregation receives them. If the congregation can't receive or respect a candidate, then he or she is probably not the person God has called to lead that particular flock.

Fourth, the candidate needs to have the capacity for problem solving executive-level issues. God surrounds power with problems so that only problem solvers will be trusted with power. Executive-level leadership also means executive-level challenges and problems! Good preaching isn't enough to be an executive leader. The ability to walk in wisdom and solve problems is one of the top qualifiers for those being considered as successors for senior pastors.

Fifth, the candidate needs to have a strong marriage and a spouse who understands the sacrificial nature of the call to lead. A church is not only retaining a senior pastor but also the spouse and children of the candidate. If the spouse is not supportive or committed to God, then the candidate should be held back until the spouse is in full agreement or in a good place with God. Nothing will derail a senior pastor quicker than having a spouse who doesn't want him or her to make sacrifices for the sake of the people and the ministry.

Sixth, the candidate needs to have a test run of being fully in charge for a season so that he or she can be truly assessed. After all is said and done, the only real way to know the capabilities of a candidate for senior pastor is to let him or her fully lead for four to six months to see how he or she does. Of course, this should be one of the last things done before moving a candidate into a senior-level role; much mentoring and preparation should have already taken place before putting him or her under that kind of pressure. If the person can handle serving in a senior leadership role for three months, then allow him or her to do it for six months and again evaluate before handing the senior role of the church over to him or her.

Seventh, the candidate needs to have the gifting to take the congregation to the next level.
A candidate should not just have administrative capacity but also the leadership capacity to take the congregation to the next level. It is not enough that the church is maintained; it is always God's will that the successor increases the productivity and fruit of the church so that the church does much greater in the second and third generation than in its first generation. This is in line with what Jesus taught us in John 14:12 and in other passages where the children enlarged the territory of the kingdom after their fathers handed it over to them. (For example, David did better than Saul and Solomon had more success than David, etc.)

Eighth, the candidate needs to be rooted and grounded in the word and spiritual disciplines.
The worst thing that can happen is to put a person in as the spiritual leader just because he or she is gifted. It is not enough to have great administrative capacity and preaching gifts. The number one requirement is to have a vast knowledge of the word and ways of God so the leader can hear the voice of God. Leaders who do not daily practice the spiritual disciplines of prayer, Bible meditation, and worship are not worth a dime.

Ninth, the candidate can't have major financial issues related to debt. Candidates who are in a lot of financial debt are dangerous because they will be tempted to compromise the word of God or do things that are unethical in order to bring in more money for income. If a person can't manage his or her home properly, then how can he or she manage the house of God (1 Tim. 3:5)?

Finally, the candidate needs to be able to manage the complexities of organizational challenges. In this day and age, it is getting harder and harder to lead a growing church. Now a senior leader has to be well versed in the basics of nonprofit rules and regulations, real estate, and business management. He or she also needs to have a high emotional intelligence to be able to relate well to people, manage a staff, hold leaders accountable, continually develop and nurture new leaders, place people in ministry according to their natural and spiritual giftings, and extract out of the church's DNA a compelling purpose that he or she can communicate and use to motivate people to give their lives for the cause of Christ. Sounds daunting, doesn't it? Well, yes, it is! That is why we need to continually pray for our senior pastors and be very careful when selecting and processing potential senior pastors.

CHAPTER 24

Seven Contrasts between Fathers and Teachers

The Bible teaches us in 1 Corinthians 4:15 that we have many teachers but not many fathers in the church. It is important to remember the significant role fathers play in the formation of both their spiritual and biological children. I speak as a man who functions in and understands both roles. (In most situations when I am speaking outside of my local church, I function as a teacher; with pastors and leaders to whom I am assigned, I function more as a father with a teaching anointing.)

I realize that we can also make a case for mothering and spiritual mothers. Because I am speaking based on personal experience, I will limit my remarks to fathering.

The following are (perhaps exaggerated) generalities to accentuate the different functions of fathers and teachers.

1. Teachers disseminate information; fathers pour out their lives.

The primary function of a teacher is to take the revelation of scripture and make it practically applicable for everyday living.

While teachers are called primarily to spend time studying and dispensing knowledge and information, fathers are primarily called to pour out their lives to those for whom they are responsible. A father's primary method of teaching is through modeling excellence and wisdom in his life for his spiritual children. Fathers go by the adage "people don't care how much you know until they know how much you care."

This is the primary method Paul used to disciple Timothy, his foremost disciple. In a summation of his discipleship method, Paul reminded Timothy of "his way of life" right before his own martyrdom (2 Tim. 4:10–11). Paul defended his apostleship by illustrating his patient endurance in the midst of suffering, not by recounting his greatest sermons (read 2 Cor. 11:16–32). Also, he not only spent for his children, but he expended himself as well (2 Cor. 12:15).

2. Teachers are motivated by illumination; fathers are motivated by personal transformation.

As a teacher in the body of Christ, I am constantly motivated to learn and understand more about the scriptures and leadership principles so that I can pass my learning on through writing and preaching. However, when it comes to those in my special circle of people that I am assigned to father, I am more motivated by seeing the teachings bear fruit for personal transformation. I am called to walk with them, correct them, encourage them, and aid them in their life journeys so they will maximize their fullest potential. It is not enough for me to teach those in this group; I need to be available to coach them in their personal lives as well.

3. Teachers search for students; fathers search for sons and daughters.

Teachers enjoy nothing so much as being in a room full of hungry students who can pull knowledge, information, and insight out of them. Those wired by God to father only view the classroom as an entrée to find potential leaders they can build relationally with.

4. We have many teachers; we do not have many fathers.

Though there are countless teachers, mentors, and coaches in the body of Christ who can edify all of us, each person is only assigned one primary father for his or her life's journey. For example, in biological families there is only one father and one mother, though a person may have grandparents, aunts, uncles, and siblings who affect his or her life.

I believe that when Paul says this in 1 Corinthians 4:15, he is also referring to the fact that so few saints in the church ever continue to mature enough in the faith to take on the role of spiritual father. After almost four decades of full-time ecclesial ministry experience, I also concur that rare indeed is this function! How sad it is that most of the pastors and leaders in the church try to replace the "way of Jesus and the apostles" with Bible institutes and schools. Formal Bible studies and education will never take the place of the model of nurturing leadership modeled in the Gospels, the book of Acts, and the epistles. One of the reasons for so much disloyalty and splitting in the church is because of a lack of fathering between senior pastors and their spiritual children, because children will resent and rebel against fathers who do not spend time with them.

I believe the primary reason many leaders in the body of Christ die unsatisfied and unfulfilled is that when they look back on their lives, they see that they have not left behind a legacy of spiritual children who will carry on their work. Achieving fame, speaking at large conferences, or writing best-selling books will never satisfy people in old age like having their children around them!

5. Teachers bask in joy at academic success; fathers enjoy life success.

Teachers are thrilled when their students do well in school and become great students of the word. Fathers realize that, just because someone is filled with knowledge and has a great grasp of biblical knowledge, there is no guarantee that person will have a successful personal life and fulfill his or her mission. John said that he had no greater joy than to find his children walking in the truth—not in his children merely having the truth (2 John 4; 3 John 4).

6. Teachers have an intellectual connection with their students; fathers have a heart connection with their children.

Teachers are stimulated when they have deep intellectual exchanges with students and congregations while teaching and preaching, or while doing question and answer sessions during informal discussions. They walk away from such encounters extremely satisfied because of the opportunity to dispense their vast knowledge. Fathers are not satisfied with such exchanges unless they also involve a long-term strategy to be involved in a process of pouring their lives into their students. This is because fathers are motivated more by a heart-to-heart connection than an exchange of the minds. Heart-to-heart connections delve into the heart, the mind, the soul, and the emotions of a person; they enable a father to penetrate beyond the surface and into the real life of a son or daughter. While a teacher may get excited when a student screams amen during a great lecture, a father desires to peer into the (compartmentalized) soul of a son or daughter with the intent to bring wholeness and integrity. This is the only way fathers' teachings can bear much fruit and bring their spiritual children to maturity.

7. Teachers desire opportunity to teach; fathers seek opportunity for their sons and daughters to minister.

Teachers bask in the opportunity to teach, even to the point where they would do it for nothing if they had to! They are always looking for a platform to get out their vast knowledge through preaching, teaching, blogging, books, CDs, DVDs, and all other forms of available media. They gauge their level of success in life by how far and wide their teachings are being heard and received by the masses. On the other hand, fathers do not gauge their success by the extent of their ministry platform but by the extent of the platform they prepare for their spiritual seed. They take greater pleasure being in the background while those they have poured into are bearing much fruit in the foreground! Instead of living for their fifteen minutes of fame, they live to wash the feet of their children and to commit their lives to their success!

Finally, while many are attempting to preach and teach a message, not too many are willing to live that message out, through those they have spent years coaching into maturity for the maximization of their potential for the glory of God and expansion of His kingdom. Oh God, give us more fathers!

CHAPTER 25

The Five Love Languages of Pastors

Every person has a love language through which he or she shows and receives affection. The following are things pastors appreciate that make up their love languages.

1. The Faithful Paying of Tithes and Offerings

A person's commitment to God is not gauged by how much he or she sings, dances, or cries in a church service or alone worshipping. This is considered merely sentimentalism toward God—not commitment—if not backed up with a financial commitment. Jesus spoke about money more than any other subject in the New Testament. All of the parables either directly or indirectly dealt with the stewardship of money and assets. This is because "where your treasure is, there your heart will be also" (Matthew 6:21). I know a person's commitment to God three ways:

    A. by seeing his or her checkbook,
    B. by viewing his or her credit card bills,
    C. by seeing how he or she uses discretionary time.

How people spend their time and money is a greater indicator of how much they love God than what they express with their mouths. For example, if a Christian spends more money on vacations and entertainment than he or she gives to the church and missions, this demonstrates that the person loves pleasure more then he or she loves the Gospel.

2. Attending Church Faithfully

Some estimate there are 25 million unchurched Evangelicals in our nation. For many it is because they were hurt in a church; others think they can have a private walk with the Lord as long as they watch Christian television and hear Gospel preaching and teaching, etc. The Bible teaches that, when we come to Christ, we become a part of His body (1 Cor. 12:12–13). Hence, whether we like the church or not, it is impossible to be saved outside of becoming a part of the church!

When we are not faithfully committed to and functioning properly in a local church or the greater body of Christ, we become dysfunctional members of the body in the same way we may have a broken foot, paralyzed hand, etc. We may still be part of the body but not a functional part (read 1 Corinthians 12).

Some folks constantly miss important church services and then tell their pastor, "I was with you in spirit, although not present in body." I tell such people, "I would rather you were with me in body because then your spirit would catch up anyway!"

To see the importance of church attendance, look no further than Acts 2:1–4, in which only the 120 people present in the upper room were filled with the Holy Spirit. The other 380 people mentioned in 1 Corinthians 15:6 missed this historic beginning of the church even if their spirits and hearts loved Jesus!

3. Volunteering Time and Service

Most churches depend on a volunteer army for the general operations of the church. For example, ushers, worship team, technical teams, Sunday school teachers, etc., are usually all unpaid volunteers.

Without a volunteer army, a church cannot possibly sustain itself and would greatly limit its membership capacity. A church can only grow commensurate with the number of faithful volunteers it can recruit and properly train.

If a person says he or she is committed to God and the church yet is not willing to volunteer time and steward his or her gifts in the context of the local church, most pastors will view that person as uncommitted both to God and the church.

4. Bringing New People to Church

The average church loses about one-third of its regular attendees annually for any number of reasons, including moving geographically away, apostasy and backsliding, being offended, not making enough friends, becoming discouraged, not connecting to the vision of the church, etc. Because of the annual average loss of people, churches are constantly under pressure to replenish their congregations with new people by about 33 percent annually to sustain their current attendance level. Because pastors generally spend most of their time ministering to the flock, they depend on the flock to recruit new members. The primary mission of the church is to win souls and make disciples. Thus, a church that doesn't encourage its members to reach out to unchurched people and evangelize is a church that is dead or dying and doesn't know it.

Furthermore, a church that has members with an average age of fifty or older and that doesn't have a plan to reach the next generation is a church without a future, even if it has a lot of attendees and members.

5. Regularly Praying for and Affirming the Pastor, Leadership, and Church Vision

Since overseeing a local church is extremely difficult, pastors greatly value those who regularly pray for them and their families. Pastors can intuit who is really praying for them and can distinguish them from those who merely say they are praying for them.

Pastors and spouses need a lot of affirmation and especially take note when congregants speak affirming words or give gifts and tokens of appreciation for all their hard work.

When I visit churches as a guest minister, I tell the congregations that if they love their families and businesses, the greatest thing they can do is fast and pray for their pastor and family. After all, as the pastor goes, so goes the local church, and as the local church goes, so goes the destiny of their families and businesses for generations to come!

Author Ministry Page

www.josephmattera.org

Other books by Joseph Mattera

Ruling in the Gates,
Kingdom Revolution,
Kingdom Awakening,
Walk in Generational Blessings
Travail to Prevail,
An Anthology of Essays on Apostolic Leadership
12 Ways to Turn Your Failure into Success

Connect with Joseph Mattera on
Facebook, Twitter and Instagram